ROBOPATHS

ROBOPATHS

Lewis Yablonsky

The Bobbs-Merrill Company, Inc.
Indianapolis · New York

To J. L. Moreno
and
to my family

CONTENTS

ACKNOWLEDGMENTS

Author and publisher are grateful to the following for permission to reprint selections over 300 words or dramatic excerpts from published works:

from *Who Shall Survive?* (1934 and 1953), *Theater of Spontaneity* (1947), *The First Psychodramatic Family* (1964), and *Psychodrama* vols. I (1970) and III (1969), by J. L. Moreno. © in the respective years indicated by J. L. Moreno and by Beacon House, Inc. Reprinted by permission.

from *R.U.R. and The Insect Play* by Karel and Josef Čapek. © 1961 by Oxford University Press. Reprinted by permission.

from "The Battle Hymn of Lt. Calley" by Julian Wilson and James M. Smith. © 1971 by Shelby Singleton Music, Inc./Quickit Publishing Co. Reprinted by permission.

from "Joey: A 'Mechanical Boy'" by Bruno Bettelheim. © 1959 by

Scientific American, Inc. Reprinted by permission. All rights reserved.

from *Inside the Third Reich* by Albert Speer, trans. Richard and Clara Winston. © 1969 by Verlag Ullstein G.m.b.h. © 1970 by the Macmillan Company. Reprinted by permission of The Macmillan Company and of George Weidenfeld & Nicholson, Ltd.

from *Joe*, screenplay by Norman Wexler. © 1970 by Cannon, Inc. Reprinted by permission of Avon Books, Inc.

from *Life in the Crystal Palace* by Alan Harrington. © 1958, 1959 by Alan Harrington. Reprinted by permission of Alfred A. Knopf, Inc. and of International Famous Agency.

from *The Trial* by Franz Kafka, trans. Edwin and Willa Muir. © 1937, 1956 and renewed 1965 by Alfred A. Knopf, Inc. Reprinted by permission of: Alfred A. Knopf; Schocken Books, Inc.; and Martin Secker & Warburg, Ltd.

from *The Stranger* by Albert Camus, trans. Stuart Gilbert. © 1942, 1946 by the estate of Albert Camus and by Alfred A. Knopf, Inc. Reprinted by permission of Alfred A. Knopf, Inc. and of Hamish Hamilton, Ltd.

from *Points of Rebellion* by William O. Douglas. © 1969, 1970 by William O. Douglas. Reprinted by permission of Random House, Inc. and of Lantz-Donadio Literary Agency.

from *Do It!* by Jerry Rubin. © 1970 by Social Education Foundation. Reprinted by permission of Simon & Schuster, Inc. and of Jerry Rubin and Jonathan Cape, Ltd.

from "The Story of Diana: The Making of a Terrorist" by Lucinda Franks and Thomas Powers. © 1971 by United Press International. Reprinted by permission.

Thanks also to the following for the use of shorter newspaper excerpts which these publishing or news service firms hold in copyright in the respective years indicated in the notes accompanying the text: Los Angeles *Times*; National Newspaper Syndicate; New York *Herald Tribune*; New York *Times*; *The Observer* (London); San Francisco *Chronicle* and *Sunday Examiner and Chronicle*; Santa Monica *Evening Outlook*; United Press International; Washington Post/Los Angeles Times News Service.

PREFACE

A WORLD WIRED FOR DEATH

The Automated Battlefield is the real revolution to come out of the Vietnam war. The possibility is that future conflicts will be fought with sensors that signal the enemy presence to computers which order air attacks from pilotless drone helicopters, or ion curtains that zap anything that steps across. With the all-Automated Battlefield, bravery becomes automatic, loyalty unquestioned, responsibility undecipherable, and the robots that roll up to join the volunteer army of the 1980's may not even care which of them is the first component to win the Medal of Honor. . . . Addressing the *Army Association* General William C. Westmoreland squinted into the future: "No more than

ten years should separate us from the Automated
Battlefield." . . . a new philosophy of war, a manless,
foolproof, giant lethal pinball machine out of which
no living thing could ever escape. The entire world,
if wired right, could become a great maze of circuitry
and weaponry, a jungle from which those who walk
off the straight paths from home to store would be
immediately and totally eliminated . . .

For several years now military money has backed
projects at Stanford Research Institute and MIT.
These efforts have gone far beyond the theoretical
stage and have developed beyond mechanical infancy.
The Stanford robot can pick out and kick over wood
blocks, and the MIT robot can distinguish between
faces. While neither robot has yet been drafted into
battle, the Department of Defense is not spending
money on these projects for nothing. The Senate
Armed Services Preparedness Investigating Subcom-
mittee, after three days of closed hearings on the subject in November, 1970, determined that $3.25
billion *had been* appropriated for the program. . . .

—SAN FRANCISCO *Chronicle*

Technocratic developments have always had two edges, one
that benefits people and another that is potentially destructive. Prior to this century, however, technology versus human
survival was not the critical issue it is today. Dr. J. L. Moreno,
a prophet of our time, raised the core question—who shall
survive, people or their machines?—over fifty years ago. This
theme of his now classic book entitled *Who Shall Survive?*
has become more significant each year as we seem to move
closer to a potential apocalypse.

Among the many pertinent observations of Moreno on
people and machines in *Who Shall Survive?* was the following haunting speculation:

The fate of man threatens to become that of the
dinosaur in reverse. The dinosaur may have perished

because he extended the power of his organism in excess of its usefulness. Man may perish because of reducing the power of his organism by fabricating robots in excess of his control.

Paradoxically, although it is increasingly a distinct possibility, the final outcome of people versus their technological robots may not be the total physical annihilation of people. People may in a subtle fashion become robot-like in their interaction and become human robots, or *robopaths*. This more insidious conclusion to the present course of action would be the silent disappearance of *human* interaction. In another kind of death, *social death*, people would be oppressively locked into robot-like interaction in human groups that had become *social machines*. In this context, the apocalypse would come in the form of people mouthing ahuman, regimented platitudes on a meaningless dead stage.

The relationship between potential *social death* and imminent megamachine wars that cause physical death is complex. A fact that can not be ignored is that it is after all the masses of people who ultimately permit their energies and financial resources to be heavily spent on ecologically suicidal technology and doomsday machines. If a majority of people in a society permit, or desire, this condition to exist they must be relatively devoid of compassion and humanistic values; or, to take a more charitable view, they have become so out of touch with reality, and have become so powerless, that they no longer exert any control over their elected acompassionate robopathic leaders.

Whatever the reasons, the people in power are actually developing the technological machinery for "a world wired for death," and a majority of the people in contemporary societies are socially dead, living a day-to-day robopathic existence.

Social death is revealed not only by the megaproblems of potential doomsday war machinery, but also by the death of compassion in a continuing series of horrendous live-movie events. Consider Attica State Prison and the senseless "fish-in-a-barrel" slaughter of thirty-five helpless people. The victims, most with their hands over their heads in surrender, were gunned down on the instructions of a governor whose atrocity was encouraged and later affirmed by the president through his vice-presidential mouthpiece. Combined, the social conditions that produce Atticas, the victims' responses, and the quality of the establishment's counterattacks reveal many aspects of the general robopathic condition.

The analysis of this *robopathic* condition of *social death*; concepts about people oppressed by technology and social machines; reaction formations and revolutionary action against these ahuman conditions; and possible solutions to these problems comprise the extravagant goals of this book.

The United States is stage center in this contemporary sociodrama of survival. America is not, however, the only country plagued by the problems focused on in this book. An examination of most societies around the world reveals that the issues delineated here are clearly international in scope.

There are no villains or heroes in this sociodrama. There are certain people, organizations, and social systems locked in ahuman postures; and there are others who are striving for a more humanistic life style.

America, in this struggle, is not in my view the doomsday "Fascist Amerika" depicted by the outraged political left, nor is it the sparkling, absolutely right system seen by the self-proclaimed super-patriots. In the great conflict of humanistic people versus their physical and social machines, America is simply the arch-protagonist of our time. America's beauty, its conflicts, and its paradoxes reveal the broader existential condition—that of people everywhere living in megamachine, plastic societies.

LEWIS YABLONSKY

California State College
Hayward, California

ROBOPATHS

1

ROBOPATHS

The term "robot" was introduced in 1923 by the Czecho-slovakian writer Karel Čapek in a play entitled *R.U.R.* The letters stand for Rossum's Universal Robots, the centerpiece of a classic science-fiction play about a factory that manufactured human-like machine robots for worldwide use.

The formula for the robots was created by an inventor named Rossum. Early in the play Rossum's son, head of the plant since his father's death, comments about his father:

> He invented a worker with the minimum amount of requirements. He had to simplify him. He rejected everything that did not contribute directly to the progress of work. In this way he rejected everything that makes man more expansive. In fact, he rejected

man and made the Robot. Robots are not people.
Mechanically they are more perfect than we are, they
have an enormously developed intelligence, but they
have no soul . . .

They've astonishing memories, you know. If you
were to read a twenty-volume Encyclopaedia to them,
they'd repeat it all to you with absolute accuracy.
But they never think of anything new.

In the story line of the play, the robots rebel against their
human masters, organize, and begin to assume power by
systematically killing off the people who created them.
Toward the end of the play the robot leaders plead for help
from a scientist who is the only human left in the world.
They desperately need his help with their central dilemma,
the problem of reproducing themselves. If they do not learn
the formula for reproduction from this scientist, they will
become extinct.

The contemporary problems of automation, megamachines, and potential ecological and social suicide have some
interesting parallels with Čapek's remarkable literary predictions. In the play, Dr. Gall, the director of the robot plant,
responds to an inquisitive woman's questions about the potential of self-destruction by the rising growth of robots. His
response parallels the commentary of many bureaucrats and
politicians on the contemporary scene.

Dr. Gall: Because the Robots are being manufactured, there's a surplus of labour supplies. So people
are becoming superfluous, unnecessary so to speak.
Man is really a survival. But that he should begin to
die out after a paltry thirty years of competition—
that's the awful part of it. You might almost think—

Helena: What?

Dr. Gall: That nature was offended at the manufacture of the Robots. . . . Nothing can be done. . . . All
the Universities in the world are sending in long peti-

tions to restrict the manufacture of the Robots. Otherwise, they say, mankind will become extinct through lack of fertility. But the R.U.R. shareholders, of course, won't hear of it. All the governments in the world are even clamouring for an advance in production, to raise the manpower of their armies. All the manufacturers in the world are ordering Robots like mad. Nothing can be done . . .

Helena: And has nobody demanded that the manufacture should cease altogether?

Dr. Gall: God forbid. It'd be a poor look-out for him.

Helena: Why?

Dr. Gall: Because people would stone him to death. You see, after all, it's more convenient to get your work done by Robots.

Helena: Oh, Doctor, what's going to become of people?

The current answer to Helena's question is that people are, as in *R.U.R.*, among other things destroying their relationship to their natural ecological environment because it is more immediately convenient to get their work done by the variety of ahuman robot machines even though this continued pattern might ultimately eliminate people. As in *R.U.R.*, people may become extinct—leaving sterile machines in their wake.

The annihilation of humanity by machines that are now in control is, as previously indicated, no longer a literary plaything. Apart from the deliberate annihilation of the "Automated Battlefield," the management of current doomsday machines seems to be slipping out of control:

A REPORT ON DOOMSDAY MACHINES

The world's political leaders are already losing control of their weapons—to computers, an international group of weapon scientists, including both Americans and Russians, will report today.

Their warning of an approaching day of Doctor Strangelove-style war—war in which programmed machines and not presidents or premiers pull the nuclear trigger—will be presented to an international scientists' assembly here. . . . The previously unpublicized weapons report is the summary of a . . . conference on new technology and the arms race . . . according to this summary, 26 experts on arms technology—including several from the Soviet Union—felt that:

There is already "growing dependence of [arms] systems on complex and rapid computer-controlled response and consequent erosion of the control of political leaders over final decision.

In the extreme, [this] could lead to systems which would be triggered on warning of attack, thereby placing the fate of the superpowers and the world entirely in the hands of radars and other sensors, and of the computers and technicians which control and interpret them.

Defining Robopaths
and the Robopathic Existence

The problem of the physical machine takeover of the destiny of people is obviously a phenomenon of enormous proportion. An even greater problem, one that is more subtle and insidious, exists. This involves the growing dehumanization of people to the point where they have become the walking dead. This dehumanized level of existence places people in roles where they are actors mouthing irrelevant platitudes, experiencing programmed emotions with little or no compassion or sympathy for other people. People with this condition suffer from the existential disease of robopathology. In a society of robopaths, violence reaches monstrous proportions, wars are standard accepted practice, and conflict abounds.

Robots are machine-made simulations of people. I would

coin the term *robopath* to describe people whose pathology entails robot-like behavior and existence. Robopaths have what Kierkegaard called "the sickness unto death." A robopath is a human who has become socially dead. Robopaths are people who function in terms of a pseudo-image. They are automatons who may appear turned on to other people but are in fact egocentric, and without true compassion. Robopaths are the reverse of Čapek's technological robots, they are people who simulate machines. Their existential state is ahuman.

There are at least eight identifiable and interrelated characteristics that may help to define the phenomenon of the robopath. These include: (1) ritualism, (2) past-orientation, (3) conformity, (4) image-involvement, (5) acompassion, (6) hostility, (7) self-righteousness, and (8) alienation.

Ritualism

Robopaths enact ritualistic behavior patterns in the context of precisely defined and accepted norms and rules. Robopaths have a limited ability to be spontaneous, to be creative, to change direction, or to modify their behavior in terms of new conditions. They are comfortable with the all-encompassing social machine definitions for behavior. Even the robopath's most emotional behavior is ritualistic and programmed. Sex, violence, hostility, recreation are all preplanned, prepackaged activities, and robopaths respond on cue. The frequency, quality, and duration of most robopaths' behavior is predetermined by societal definition.

This condition perpetuates an existence where people do not use their humanistic capacities. Their activities are rote and dreamlike in quality. Social interaction is a dull routine that has limited intellectual or emotional meaning.

Past-orientation

Robopaths are oriented to the past—rather than to the here-and-now situation, or to the future. In this regard they suffer from cultural lag. They are often responding to situations and conditions that are no longer relevant or functional. They have impaired and limited vision for future emergencies. If they are locked into a behavioral pattern, they will follow the same path even though it may ultimately be self-destructive.

A deadly example of this condition is the continued use of the internal combustion gasoline automobile as a means of transportation. The evidence is overwhelming that people are dying slowly and some rapidly from smog. Yet there is no fundamental modification of the escalation of the social system that perpetuates this deadly condition. The robopaths in charge of the deadly automobile-producing machines and the oil companies are more concerned with profits than with human life; and the people who buy and drive these automotive death machines are powerless to change their susceptibility to the auto industry's powerful and seductive advertising that feeds their egos. Driving the right "in" car is more important than the death machines' ecological impact.

Conformity

Robopaths have limited spontaneity or creativity. J. L. Moreno defines spontaneity and creativity in interaction as "a new response to an old situation and an adequate response to a new situation." Robopaths are unable to be creative in old situations or to change direction for new situations.

In a robopathic-producing social machine, *conformity* is a virtue. New or different behavior is viewed as strange and bizarre. "Freaks" are feared. Originality is suspect. Consequently, the social system is seldom geared to fostering or developing a person's ability to be spontaneous and creative.

Image-involvement

Robopaths are "other-directed" rather than "inner-directed." In David Riesman's terms they are attempting to determine what is appropriate as defined by the status definition and rules provided by those around them rather than by having any inner radar or principles to determine their behavior. They are constantly attempting to be super-conformists. Their presentation of self is geared to others rather than to any self principles. They have limited or no interior definition for their behavioral enactments. Their behavior is thus dominated by image or status requirements set by the surrounding society.

Acompassion

If compassion entails a true concern for the human interests of others, at times at one's personal expense, robopaths are acompassionate. Their enactments are generally neither against other people or for other people in terms of a sense of personal moral values or principles. They act—essentially in terms of what is most expedient behavior to further or conform with their expected status or image in the social system. They will thus most often conform to the rules and the expectations of the majority.

They do not have any humanistic values that dictate or define their behavior. In this sense they are neither compassionate nor non-compassionate. They are *without* any compassionate values or social conscience. They will act out their role "properly" regardless of the destructive impact it may have on other people. Their role and its "proper" enactment becomes paramount over any concern for other people.

The grotesque consequences of programmed acompassion are found in the "silent majority" of Germany's response to the Nazi regime's butchery; and more recently the powerlessness of people to stop the daily starvation and death of thousands of Biafran children. The mass society robopath mentality provides limited opportunity for compassionate action on such problems.

Hostility

Hostility both *covert* and *overt* is a significant characteristic of a society of robopaths and is a quality found in robopathic people. People unable to act out their spontaneity and creativity develop repressed, venomous pockets of hostility. In some robopathic roles, as for example soldier, there is a built-in escape valve for the aggressive build-up that would emerge from being a number in a war machine. The soldier can kill the enemy. Many bureaucrats also often have an acceptable structure for ventilating their hostility on other people. They can use the rules to deny others things they desire (e.g., "The rules do not permit . . ." "We regret we can't deliver . . ." etc.)

Robopaths can also ventilate their hostility more openly. There are innumerable cases of violent homicidal outbursts by people who have been "model citizens" or "model students" and who explode dramatically (e.g., Charles Whitman, who killed fifteen people and wounded thirty-four more from a tower at the University of Texas; Charlie Starkweather, the "good boy" who killed nine people; the nice quiet man who is accused of the murder of around twenty-five migrant farm workers; et al.)

One vehicle through which the average robopath can indirectly act out his or her enormous hostility is to elect to power political leaders who are *for* "law and order," "keeping people in their place," "capital punishment," "winning the war," and generally perpetuating the conditions of dissent that produce violent outcomes.

Social death is akin to physical death. Robopathic people whose lives and interactions lack humanism are emotionally dead. Their responses to war, suffering, even the physical death of others, are basically acompassionate, even though they may overtly appear to "care." This sophisticated and dissolute pattern of alienation seems to be another symptom of the robopathic existence.

The robopathic, acompassionate response to hostility and
violence is related to Camus's *The Rebel*, where he deals
with the issue of death as a prosaic condition in which homicide and the "sanctified value of life" have become "a bore" to
the masses. Camus writes:

> The poets themselves, confronted with the murder
> of their fellow men, proudly declare that their hands
> are clean. The whole world absentmindedly turns its
> back on these crimes; the victims have reached the
> extremity of their disgrace: they are a bore. In ancient
> times the blood of murder at least produced a religious
> horror and in this way sanctified the value of life. The
> real condemnation of the period we live in is, on the
> contrary, that it leads us to think that it is not blood-
> thirsty enough. Blood is no longer visible; it does not
> bespatter the faces of our pharisees visibly enough.
> This is the extreme of nihilism; blind and savage mur-
> der becomes an oasis, and the imbecile criminal seems
> positively refreshing in comparison with our highly in-
> telligent executioners.

The mass robopathic response to Lt. Calley's My Lai war
crimes reveals, in part, the increasingly ahuman response to
death. The "highly intelligent" political executioners continue their remote killing—partly because of the apathy of
the masses of robopaths.

This theme of moral corruption and the mass acompassionate acceptance of death and violence has found its way
into many recent art forms. For example, in a film called
Hard Contract, a hired killer (the story never discloses his
employer) sits casually in a theater munching a candy bar.
He is calmly watching a newsreel portraying a war in Africa
which shows the bloated, dying bodies of starving children.
A news commentator on the screen is unemotionally specu-
lating on the statistically predictable deaths of several
thousand more children, future victims of seemingly uncontrollable war and starvation. In the midst of this impersonal

human holocaust, the robopathic killer (everyman) in the audience leans over and quietly kills his victim-of-the-month. The audience (and everyone is part of this audience) is confronted with the questions: which is more horrible, the inexorable murders on the screen or the murder in the theater? Is one any more real than the other? The total film message suggests that perhaps the mass of people may have quietly broken through the ahuman barrier into the acompassionate acceptance of violence, including homicide. The film implies that the general public is no longer horrified by violence and accepts hostility. It has become an integral part of the new robopathic, acompassionate human condition. People who in the extreme are the socially dead, ahuman participants in the machine society, may have quietly slipped into this phase where natural death, or even murder, has become commonplace and accepted. The mass acceptance of hostility and violence may be the ultimate acompassionate characteristic of the condition of a mass alienation from life.

Self-righteousness

Robopathic behavior is super-conformist. It is never deviant or against the norms of the social machine. Consequently, the robopath's behavior is always "right" or considered self-righteous. The robopath's inner equilibrium is seldom disturbed by guilt or anxiety because he is attuned to expectations of the social machine.

Adolf Eichmann (a classic robopathic hero), for example, was most self-righteous about carrying out the job of exterminating undesirables. He had no time to concern himself with any inner guilt or turmoil about his role. Efficiency was the keynote.

In a similar vein, as mentioned, Lt. Calley's routine killing of "oriental civilians," even after the details of the horrendous crime were made public, produced a mass affirmation of his behavior by a robopathic majority. (One mass poll revealed that 75 percent of the population disapproved of his conviction.) Interestingly, the "righteousness" of his incredible acts was affirmed by "church leaders." The atrocious behavior was "righteous" to the robopathic majority because it was committed under the banner of Americanism; just as the extermination of Jews was righteously carried out in the interest of Nazi Germany.

In a broader context many efficient robopathic parents are self-righteous about the cold and highly defined discipline they inflict on their children. As robopathic parents administer a spanking (or worse, as demonstrated by horrendous child-battering cases) they will cite certain Biblical admonitions about sin or "correct behavior." They will literally whip their children into conformist shape—so that they are not embarrassed in front of the neighbors by certain immoral profanity, sexual references, or "bad behavior" that negatively affects their image. They self-righteously believe they are doing the correct thing. In effect, they build their children into robopathic people in their own image.

Alienation

Despite the general overall appearances of "togetherness," the typical robopath is in effect alienated from *self, other people,* and the *natural environment.* He or she is alienated from *self* in the sense that his or her ego is only a function of ritualistic demands—it has no intrinsic self-definition. It is a component of a social machine.

Robopaths are alienated from *other people* because their interaction with others is usually in terms of "others" as *objects,* not *human beings.* They are role-objects like children, employees, employers, another body on a bus or train, another object in the anonymous crowd. There is limited room for compassion toward objects.

A grotesque example of this kind of alienation is the robopathic onlooker response to the public murder of Kitty Genovese in New York City. Thirty-nine people stood by and watched this object-victim Kitty Genovese as she was stabbed

to death by an assailant and were not sufficiently impelled to
respond in any way to prevent her death.

Another example of this quality of alienation is observable
in many salesmen as robopathic role-players. Many salesmen
have limited compassion and are *alienated* from their clients
or customers as human beings. To such salesmen the customers are not human, they are objects to be strategically
manipulated for profit. Although ethical considerations are
part of the veneer of the salesmen's role, in practice they will
sell their *product* "by any means necessary" (e.g., a recent
government report listed 369 highly advertised drug products
that were either useless or hazardous. One of the most heavily
"sold" products is, of course, carcinogenic, death-dealing to-
bacco). The financial profit motive dehumanizes salesmen
and their clients by alienating or isolating these role-players
from any humanistic interaction as people. The inter-actors
become robopathic objects to each other in their ahuman
interaction.

Robopaths are *alienated* from their *natural environment*,
because they pay more attention to the plastic intervening
variables of their social machines than to the natural spectacle
that surrounds them. Moreover, their ritualistic, locked-in
position and behavior is a methodical destroyer of the natural
ecological conditions of earth. Robopaths rape the earth,
the air, the water, and other natural resources without com-
punction in the *normal* course of their behavior.

ROBOPATHOLOGY

Every historical period seems to have its dominant social-
psychological pathology. Robopathology may be the classic
disease of this era.

Freud determined that neurosis was the central emotional
disorder of his time. In gross terms psychosis, sociopathology,
and neurosis have been widespread and significant disorders

of the post-World War II period. The twenty-first century may be characterized by an epidemic of robopathology.

This behavioral syndrome has always been in some degree a destructive side effect of technological systems. As technocracies and "technological progress" accelerate, the side effect correlative impact on people appears to be a marked increase in robopathology.

The pathology is already rampant and may in time eclipse the other identifiable behavioral disorders. Robopathic behavior and existence is less apparent, more difficult to identify, and therefore more insidious, than the other maladies. It appears to be a built-in part of a technocratic system.

Robopaths are efficient functionaries and bureaucrats. They meld into social machines, as functional cogs, in part because as Čapek stated, "they never think of anything new and they have no soul."

Robopaths are not deviants. They super-conform to the dictates of megamachines. In this regard they commit subtle ahuman and dehumanizing acts as a normative part of an overall system that expects limited human compassion. In the extreme, robopaths are agents who perpetuate, validate, and commit acts of social death.

In this regard robopaths are like "white-collar criminals" who are not really legally considered criminals, and have no self-concept of being deviant. White-collar criminals are individuals who commit their crimes in the *normal* course of their business activities in a corporate entity. They have no self-definition of being criminal and in fact are seldom prosecuted by the society or people against whom they commit their acts. Very often they are highly respected and admired members of the community. Their legal criminality does, however, erode the moral quality of the society; and this is more destructive in total than all of traditional crime combined. In a similar way robopathic behavior erodes the humanistic quality of a society and is therefore more destructive than all other behavior disorders combined.

A subtle characteristic of robopathology is that (like other diseases) it is not an *all-or-none* phenomenon. There are always degrees of pathology. An infected limb may or may not affect the total physiological system of a person. Also there are obviously degrees of intensity of infection. In a parallel way the infected person or social system may have a partially compartmentalized condition. An individual may have a full, happy, humanistic family situation and slave in a robopathic occupation role for the other half of his life. Or the reverse may be true; the individual's home life style is a robopathic existence. He "labors" in his relationship with his wife and child. The wife detests her robopathic housewife existence. They mouth platitudes of "relating" and "togetherness." Their sex life is a prescribed meaningless ritual they were taught to statistically experience. In another area of his life, his job turns him on. In this role he is spontaneous, creative, and is carrying out work that is compassionate and meaningful for himself and other people.

Robopathology often emerges when people in standard socialization process societies *cop out* or *sell out* their humanistic drives of excitement, joy, and courage to the cultural press of social machines because of fear and often an instilled sense of inadequacy. They often trade their more spontaneous creative potentials for familiar regularized rituals. In this way they avoid putting themselves to any test where they might be judged or emerge as inferior. In the processes of a dehumanized society they live in familiar, routine, and predictable patterns of behavior. Thus they *cop out* on their humanistic motivations and become part of the social machine.

People out of their profound fear of the unknown may have created machine and social artifacts that render them impotent in terms of their natural spontaneity and creativity. They trade their spontaneity and courage for the security of a robot role with the built-in approval of being stylish or "in."

Paradoxically, in this regard, many (seemingly spontaneous) "hip," "in," or "beautiful" people are outrageous robopaths. Their time is consumed determining the latest "in" fashions.

They will acquire the "in" material objects or clothes (whether or not they can afford them) because they must maintain the fashion image—which provides them with immediate gratification, temporal identity, and a refuge from the necessity of confronting life's realities. Being "in" is an acceptable shield from being oneself, and if the "in" robopaths slavishly conform they achieve automatic approval.

Their "hip" involvement with all the fashionable nametags enables other "in" people to recognize immediately that they are O.K. Given this, there are no additional requirements—such as humanistic actions—required from the image roleplayer. This accounts, in part, for the unbelievably dull, flat quality of life in the places or situations where the "in" people congregate. Most of the interaction revolves around a series of acknowledgments regarding who is wearing what, going where, or acquiring "it." Of greatest importance is *the correct image rather than the human being.* (The "in" people's robopathic acompassion is most manifest in their snobbery and disdain for squares and others who do not play the "in" game in the right place.)

In their "image-trap," certain meeting places or "clubs" are fantastically "in" one month and "out" the next. The same is true of rapidly changing fashion. The "in" robopath is a veritable slave to the image-movie that is the rage of the moment, and other people do not count. In the extreme situation, other people are only desirable when they affirm the validity of the image presented.

Robopathic "in" people are generally lacking in spontaneity and creativity in their verbal interaction and communication with others. Most have a frozen repertoire of conversation. When they are "running their story," it may even be charming and intelligent. The problem is that it is often the only "story" they have. After it has been delivered, or if they are pressed for elaboration, they have no spontaneity or creativity to enlarge the scope of their image-presentation. In this context their human script is frozen into a robopathic act that may be clever on the surface—but remains dead at its center.

In the robopathic "image-trap" transiency is characteristic. After the "in-groupies" deliver their repertoire of wit and fashion they must move on to other groups or persons. Their frozen act no longer produces rave notices from the old audience and they need a new group. This is especially true of the playboy and playgirl robopath in their love affairs. After their act has been presented, the next step is human intimacy. Most of these people fear a humanistic level of interaction. They are either inadequate to function at this next level or they fear being found out as the shallow persons they are.

In another dimension of the robopathic phenomenon, many creative people are often corrupted by the rewards of the plastic society. They find a groove and freeze in it. For example, many innovators—writers, theorists, teachers, architects, artists—after an initially courageous and creative productive life cop out and become robopathic in their later creative attempts. They find a successful mold, receive their rewards, and ritualistically stick to it for the rest of their lives. They no longer put themselves "in harm's way" by branching out or trying a new and different approach. Their fears and lack of courage freezes them into static, uncreative roles, where they lock into a robopathic existence.

In contrast, there are many creative giants, for example, J. L. Moreno, Leonardo da Vinci, Albert Einstein, Bertrand Russell, and others, who did *not* cop out. These creative geniuses went from one successful creation or discovery to another. They lived creative, self-actualized existences all of their lives.

Most people in later life, however, attempt to acquire security in their job, their family, and their human relations. When they develop a social ploy or a game that works, they cling to it—often desperately. The price they pay is to become robopathic and to give up a part of their humanism. They become a mechanical part of the machine (art, organization, idea, or whatever) that they originally created.

Robopathology is, therefore, a complex phenomenon. It is

a condition that can afflict people of all ages and in all positions in the society. Some roles in a society are more prone to robopathology than others, and some societies have more robopathic roles than others.

Humanistic
AND ROBOT ROLES

A role is a prescribed status or position in a social system that has certain specified rights, duties, and obligations. Some statuses—for example, those of artist, musician, executive, or parent—have considerable latitude and room for creative role-playing expression. These I would term *humanistic roles*.

Other roles have a very limited range for humanistic expression, spontaneity, creativity, and compassionate action. These include such roles as assembly-line worker, file clerk, typist, and other statuses or positions circumscribed by the system. These I would term *robot roles*.

The droll monotony, boredom, and dehumanizing quality of a *robot role* is exemplified by the daily monotony of work on an assembly line in a factory. The *robot role* occupants rise at the same time, go through their ritualized breakfast, turn the screws at work, watch T.V., make ritualistic love on a prescribed night, take their two-week vacation—and become increasingly frustrated and bored by their routinized life style. Increasingly their zest for life, and capacity for spontaneity and creativity, is reduced to zero. One common consequence of this malaise is a simmering, underlying feeling of hostility and aggression toward others.

Another general example of role-type that fits the robot-role model would be a lower-level career soldier. The army "manual" or "by-the-book" is their God in terms of regulating their lives and the lives of their colleagues. Their daily routine is highly defined. There is very little spontaneity, creativity, or change of direction in their interaction with others. Their perception of the world is from the circumscribed view of the service. Also, although their avowed goals are peace and defense—they are trained to kill. In their case their simmering hostility emanating from their humanistic repression has a legitimized avenue for ventilation. They can legally kill on the battlefield. People in other robot roles are restricted to subtle and more limited acts of aggression.

In the army robot role even "loyalty" and "patriotism" are packaged and programmed by the army social machine. For example, many conscripted soldiers (involuntary role-occupants) who participate in war often question regular army men (voluntary role-occupants) about the philosophical meaning or validity of the war and killing. The latter consider the question either humorous or unpatriotic. It is humorous to hear anyone question a given *factual situation*. The response to any questions of this type is phrased one way or another in the platitude, "yours is not to question why, yours is just to do or die." In some extreme cases compassionate questioners are given hazardous assignments that might easily insure their deaths in combat.

In another facet of robopathic army behavior, American soldiers at My Lai and in other Vietnam atrocity situations killed human beings, young and old, "the gook enemy," without identifying them as people. Calling people "gooks" puts them in the position of ahuman objects. This stereotyping combined with the training of men to become robopathic, unfeeling killers is a significant part of the *social death* of war.

In contrast with robot roles, *humanistic roles* provide a greater latitude for creative self-expression. The roles of artist, teacher, parent, actor, writer, scientist, at least in terms of structural content, provide the opportunity for the role-occupants to be more spontaneous, creative, tuned into nature, and capable of leading a more humanistic way of life.

It is important to note that *robot* and *humanistic* roles can be severely modified by the role-occupant. Role-occupants, depending on their personality, can break through the role straitjacket even though it is more difficult in a *robot role* than in a *humanistic role*.

For example, some people occupying robot roles add a dimension of creativity and spontaneity to what they do and overcome the doldrums of action. They inject some novel, different, or creative dimension into their expected acting out. They commit themselves to find out more about their role's relationship to the world around them. An example is the dying breed of factory workers who were political activists in the thirties. They read and studied about the labor movement and economic theories. Their worker role was vibrant and alive, unlike most modern assembly-line factory workers or hard-hat construction workers.

In the converse, certain humanistic and creative roles can be enacted in a dehumanized dead fashion by the role-occupant. For example, a psychiatrist or psychotherapist role has a humanistic status and quality. It can, however, be enacted by a robopath role-occupant who maintains a dead, social-machine relationship with a patient. The duet of psychiatrist and patient can follow the theoretical procedural book in a dull, nonproductive, irrelevant, and ahuman fashion.

In summary, a role-occupant may breathe life into a *robot role* and the occupant of a *humanistic role* may act out in a robot-like fashion. (For example, a "creative artist" who keeps repeating and reproducing his past original work.)

The degree of robot-like behavior is thus a function of both the role and the person occupying the role. Humanistic societies would tend to have a higher number and degree of *humanistic roles* and *people*; and megamachine societies a greater number of *robot roles, robopaths,* and built-in conditions for a robopathic existence.

ROBOPATHIC PATTERNS

A significant quality of robopathology is the fact that it is insidious. It can creep into a humanistic group like a family and subtly dehumanize it by turning it into a social machine.

In thousands of psychodrama and group therapy sessions I

have directed (since 1949), I have observed the phenomenon of families as social machines. The original, loving, compassionate relationship of husband and wife becomes converted into a ritualized interaction between two robopaths who talk to each other's images and even make love in a set formula of physical action. The parents (and the children rapidly fall in line) never really communicate—or express any spontaneous, creative, or different ways of relating. This factor, more than any other, accounts for the escalation of various drop-out cultural alternatives.

In one particular example, a father encountered his son in a role-playing session about his son's "hippie tendency" and use of drugs. The father's enactment in the session was right out of a model "Father Knows Best" television drama. He woodenly expressed "compassion" for his son's health, but was more spontaneous and self-righteous in portraying his real concern about the potential irreparable damage to the family's image if the son was ever arrested. The father's performance was marked by an almost total lack of real compassionate emotion, and the son responded in kind.

After several weeks of sessions the father finally broke out of his robopathic armor, got down on his knees, and poured out sixteen years of repressed tears and emotions toward his son. He told him about his beautiful feelings for him when he was born, apologized for seldom spending time with him, admitted his hostilities, and asked the son to forgive him. The son wept and embraced his father and repeated his new discovery about his parent, "Dad, you can feel, Dad, you can feel. . . ."

The mother joined in on the session and for the first time in over sixteen years of physical intimacy the family became emotionally intimate. They broke out of the robopathic role-playing of their family social machine and began to communicate in a humanistic way.

Robopathic patterns are manifest in other group situations that traditionally, like the family, are considered to be humanistic entities. For example, even in the traditionally humanistic role of teaching there are robopathic professors who parade their ancient yellow notes, that have limited relevance or meaning, before students who in robot-like precision write them down and at the end of the term regurgitate the frozen material on examinations.

Also, in the practice of medicine, which is generally considered a humanistic system, there are robopathic doctors who diagnose by rote those familiar and convenient medical diseases which they feel they can cure. The patient has no human qualities. It (the patient) is an inert numerical form into which they ritualistically stick their finger (and other instruments) and make *acompassionate* diagnoses.

Perhaps the ultimate act of a robopathic doctor occurred in the following situation. A patient consulted the doctor about a particular ailment. He referred the patient to a clinic for a series of tests. About three weeks later, the patient, because he had not heard from the doctor, called him about the results. The dialogue between the doctor and patient reflects his robopathic posture:

Doctor: Didn't my nurse call you?

Patient: No.

Doctor: Oh, I see. Well, the tests reveal that you will be dead in from four to six weeks.

Robopathic leaders

There are many other robopathic roles in plastic societies, especially in government. Political robopathic leaders are more apparent than robopaths in the general population since they have more power and inflict more ahuman damage either by commission or omission. Consider, for example, the potent and paradoxical action of a president who claimed to "save lives"—by widening an already absurd war through sending troops into a neutral country adjacent to the "enemy's" country. Such robopathic political role-players are essentially involved with status image (their historical role), the acompassionate pressures of military robopaths, self-righteousness, and a "past-oriented" atavistic notion that regresses to a historical period when wars could be won.

For example, the absurd tragedy of the Vietnam War has been continued essentially by robopathic image considerations. Such patently absurd platitudes as "retreat with honor" and the presentation of a cardboard concept of "Vietnamization" are offered as reasons for perpetuating the killings. The robopathic leaders of the Vietnam War are like the robopathic religious leaders in Arthur Miller's play, The Crucible. After a long period of senseless butchery they secretly admit that the women they had hanged and burned were not witches. Nevertheless they feel compelled to continue to kill witches because they have already killed a sizable number and they could not openly admit the absurdity of their past behavior. Facing this reality would require the confrontation of their role as senseless killers. Robopathic leaders are inflexible to humanistic changes in direction when their self-righteous images are at stake.

In another case, one particular political action of a California governor illustrates the potential destructive impact of an ahuman robopathic politician. This robopath, an actor, was heavily involved with image status (namely reelection), and seemed to exhibit a simmering hostility toward people, especially those who are poor and in minority positions. The processes of the governmental social machine he directed were more important than any concern for the poor and minority group people, whose medical problems were escalated by this governor's robopathic role-playing.

One month after he was reelected by his constituents it was revealed that the state had an enormous deficit that curiously had been obscured by some complex bookkeeping manipulations. To maintain his image with the taxpayers who had elected him (and might elect him president) he promised that there would be no tax increases. It was also unthinkable for him to get the deficit funds from ensconced corporate entities, like oil companies, or corporate organizations that had helped finance his election; or through additional taxes from the robo-pathic majority of the citizenry that had elected him.

Instead, in an effort to make up the funds, the governor, by his actions, raped the poor, the aged, the disadvantaged, the emotionally disordered, and other minority groups. This robo-pathic leader's assault on physically sick, poor people is a classic example of the problem of white-collar robopathic criminal violence. The event and some of its consequences were, in part, summarized in the following news report:

> The full story of the Administration's third major Medi-crisis in three years, resulting in a 10 percent reduction in physicians' fees, had been slowly un-folding.
> And by last week, the plight of the patients, and the bitter realization of a drastic reduction in such "non-essential" services as psychiatric care, eye examina-tions, prosthetic devices and drugs, had aroused a storm of professional and public indignation.
> At an emergency meeting of the Medical Society, called by clinic chiefs, city officials and hospital ad-ministrators, the dreary assessment was made that:
> Patients who needed care might not be admitted to hospitals unless they were in *imminent danger of dying.* [In fact, many people, including infants, later suffered or died as a direct result of the governor's rule. One example was that of a four-month-old baby who was refused admission to a hospital on the grounds of this policy. Lacking professional care, the child subsequently died of a respiratory ailment.]
> Urgent medical operations might have to be post-poned for three, six or even nine months.
> Thousands of patients who had just begun receiving the benefits of dignified private medical care would be forced back into charity clinics that were already over-crowded.
> Drugs would have to be rationed to the poor, and many would be impossible to obtain even if a doctor wanted to prescribe them. . . .
> If not canceled, the new bureaucratic procedures

may lead to "irreparable injury, including serious illness and the threat of death" to some of the state's
2.4 million Medi patients.

This ahuman pattern that inheres within the system is not
simply bureaucratic mismanagement, or dishonesty, it is only
one example of a governmental social machine that is involved
with status maintenance (staying in office) as governor, and
involvement with the machinery of interaction rather than
the human needs of people. It is difficult to counteract social
problems when the "doctors" (in this case, the governor) are
a significant part of the overall disease of robopathology.
This case-example fits the robopath model in several respects. The people with limited status (poor people and minority groups) are futher dehumanized by a governmental
social machine that is more concerned with status-mainten-
ance than with people. The governor-leader does not deserve
all of the responsibility for the ahuman act, he merely was
acting in accord with the underlying dictates of the constituents who voted for him. He apparently was the *robopathic
model leader* desired, and he was locked into acting as he did
within the framework of an acompassionate government
social machine. In a certain sense he helped vent the spleen of
untold numbers of robopaths in the state who seem to derive
some subtle satisfaction from this governmental, social-
machine assault on powerless people.

THE COMMON ROBOPATH

Political leader robopaths of the type described are followed,
venerated, supported, and sustained by a great mass of people
who are often referred to as the "average man" or the "silent
majority." This category comprises the mass of robopaths in a
social machine.

There has been a modest amount of research into the dimensions of the common robopathic quality in relation to its
widespread manifestations. One fascinating set of experiments

that fits into this category was the research of psychologist Stanley Milgram at Yale University in the early 1960s.

In his studies Milgram was concerned with the conditions under which people would be obedient or disobedient to authority. In his overall project, during a period of several years, almost a thousand adults were subjects of his research. He investigated a variety of experimental settings and variable modifications. The results, however, were frighteningly uniform. On the basis of his research Milgram concluded that a majority of "good people," who in their everyday lives were responsible and decent, could be made to perform "callous and severe" acts on other people when they were placed in situations that had the "trappings of authority."

The "harsh acts" included giving electric shocks to another individual who might have just died of a heart attack. The following detailed example of one of Milgram's projects more graphically illustrates the general research approach that was used.

The subjects in this prototype example of the Milgram experiments on obedience were a random sample of New Haven adult males who came to Milgram's Yale Research Center in response to a newspaper advertisement. They were paid by the hour and individually brought to a laboratory and introduced to their partners who were, in reality, members of the research team. Each was then incorrectly told that he was going to participate in a learning experiment with his partner. One of them was to be the "teacher" and the other the "learner." It was contrived that the subject always wound up as the teacher, and the research assistant always became the learner. The subject was incorrectly told that the research was being conducted to determine the effects of punishment on learning.

The subject, now the teacher, witnessed the standard procedure by which the learner (in reality a member of the research staff) was strapped into a chair that apparently had electrical connections. The subject was then taken into another room and told to ask the learner certain questions from a questionnaire he was given. The teacher was told to admin-

ister electric shocks every time the learner gave a wrong answer. (In some cases, before the learner was strapped into his
electric chair, he would comment, "Take it easy on me, I
have a heart condition.")

In the room with the teacher was another member of the
research team who served as an authority figure and as a
provocateur. He was present to make sure that the subject
administered the proper shocks for incorrect answers.

The subject was told by the authority figure to give progressively stronger shocks to the learner when the latter's
answers were incorrect. In front of the subject was an elaborate
electric board that, as far as the subject knew, controlled shock
levels from 15 to 450 volts in 15-volt gradations. The last two
switches were ominously labeled **XXX**.

The researcher in the room would admonish the subject to
increase the shock for each incorrect answer. In a short time
the subject was repeatedly, as far as he knew, giving shocks
of up to 450 volts to another person in the next room. The
"victim" would often dramatically pound the wall and shout
"Stop it, you're killing me!" Some subjects balked at continuing, but proceeded on the orders of the researcher in the
room, who would simply say, "Continue the experiment."

At a certain point the "victim," after pounding on the wall,
would "play dead," or act as if he had passed out, and make
no sound. The researcher in the room would instruct the subject to count "no response" as an incorrect answer. He would
then order him to continue to shock an apparently inert or
dead body with heavy electric shocks.

In several cases when the subject refused to act out his
robopathic behavior of continuing to shock the victim because "Christ, I don't hear him anymore, maybe I killed him!
You know he said he had a bad heart," the researcher would
say, "go on with the experiment." The authoritative voice of
the *Yale* researcher caused more than half of the subjects to
continue to robopathically shock what might very well have
been a dead body!

In a part of the experiment, some subjects refused to go on.
The researcher would tell the subject to continue, and say,

"Go ahead, I'll be responsible for what happens to the 'learner.' " When this was done the subject would usually say, "O.K., I'll continue. Remember you're responsible, not me!" One of Milgram's experiments, conducted with forty subjects, is typical of those overall experiments carried out with almost one thousand people. All forty subjects complied by shocking their "victims" with up to 300 volts. Fourteen stopped at that point or at slightly higher levels. But the majority—twenty-six subjects—continued to administer increasingly more severe shocks until they reached 450 volts. This was beyond the switch marked *Danger: Severe Shock*. Thus sixty-five percent of this representative sample of "good people," paid a few dollars an hour, conformed to the dictates of an experimental authority situation to the point that *they supposedly inflicted severe pain or possible death on another human being.*

Essentially the research validated the assumption that people would conform to the dictates of people in authority even when they knew they were inflicting severe harm on another person, up to and beyond homicide. Authority, in a legitimate social context, thus produced obedience and conformity to ahuman goals: even in America!

It would be difficult to measure the degree of robopathic components in an individual, and perhaps even more difficult to estimate the number of robopathic individuals in a society. (A wild speculation, in accord with the Milgram experiment, would be: more than half of the population.) Perhaps even more difficult is the measurement of the number of what Jules Feiffer calls "little murders" that robopaths "just doing their job" inflict on people in everyday life. These "little murders" parallel the milder electric shocks in the experiment.

Several issues are blatantly clear. The majority of people tend to support illegal and immoral wars and their concomitant killings. Common robopaths do sanction many little murders and big murders, especially *if the perpetrators are legitimately acting within the proper formal societal contexts.*

The commission and allowance of human atrocities by

common robopaths is not restricted, therefore, to the commission and omissions of the much-cited prototype example of the vast majority of Germans during the Nazi regime. The phenomenon is widespread and has occurred in many eras, and in many other societies. In some measure common robopaths and their leaders must derive some perverse underlying emotional benefits from such ahuman behavior.

Literary works abound with descriptive appraisals of the condition of "common people," their proclivity for ahuman acts, and their general simmering hostility. One perceptive literary analyst of this genre of the "silent majority" of robopaths was the brilliant novelist, Nathanael West, who revealed some dimensions of the problem. In the late thirties he came to Hollywood and trained his literary camera not on the movie studios or the stars, but on the "common people" who, as West's central character in *The Day of the Locust* states, "came to California to die." West, through this character, wrote:

> All their lives they had slaved at some kind of dull, heavy labor, behind desks and counters, in the fields and at tedious machines of all sorts, saving their pennies and dreaming of the leisure that would be theirs when they had enough. Finally that day came. . . . Where else should they go but California, the land of sunshine and oranges?
> Once there, they discover that sunshine isn't enough. . . . Nothing happens. They don't know what to do with their time. . . . Their boredom becomes more and more terrible. They realize that they've been tricked and burn with resentment. . . . Nothing can ever be violent enough to make taut their slack minds and bodies. They have been cheated and betrayed. They have slaved and slaved for nothing.

In *The Day of the Locust* a central character is Tod Hackett, a young painter who is planning a painting called "The Burning of Los Angeles." (Interestingly, this artistic and literary speculation is already a reality.) The book ends with the "living dead" masses venting their frustration and hostility in a mad riot of fire that sets off the burning of other cities throughout the country. West, like Moreno, Čapek, Huxley, and Orwell, has turned out to be a seer of an incipient apocalypse nurtured by robopathic leaders and followers in contemporary social machine societies.

2

THE EMERGENCE OF ROBOPATHOLOGY AND RELATED SYNDROMES

During the Vietnam war soldiers in the first platoon of Charlie Company, First Battalion, Twentieth Infantry of the American Army swept into the Vietnamese hamlet of My Lai. They left in their wake hundreds of dead civilians, including women and children. Several small children with bullet-punctured diapers were later photographed lying dead in the dust.

The perpetrators of this horrendous act, later legally defined as a war crime, were not psychotics or psychopaths, but a representative sample of typical American young men, most of whom had been involuntarily drafted into the army. One of the American soldiers who participated in the killings that day later commented:

> You know when I think of somebody who would
> shoot up women and children, I think of a real nut,
> a real maniac, a real psycho; somebody who has just
> completely lost control and doesn't have any idea
> of what he's doing. That's what I figured. That's what
> I thought a nut was. Then I found out [at My Lai]
> that an act like, you know, murder for no reason, that
> could be done by just about anybody.

The young men at My Lai were apparently not too different from the typical Americans in the Milgram experiments who, under orders, shocked people (from their perception) to their death. Nor were they apparently very different from the spectators who passively played their spectator role of watching people being murdered, as did the thirty-nine robopathic people who felt no obligation to intervene in the stabbing to death of Kitty Genovese. They were also representatives of the powerless silent majority who are unquestioningly supporting over $3 billion in research that may ultimately lead to "a world wired for death."

The point is that the robopathic response which can be an act of commission or omission can be built-in to people in so-called "civilized" social systems. People can be, and apparently are, subtly trained to "carry out orders" or play their roles even when such orders or roles entail horrendous acts. The acts I am referring to are acts without compassion. Acts which more or less kill other people.

These robopathic-acompassionate acts are not always deadly. There are levels of acompassionate murder that can run anywhere from the unwarranted small biting sarcasm to the ultimate act of homicide.

The rationalization or self-justification for attacks (small or large) on humanity are generally found in the context of the system. Eichmann's classic comment about "only doing his job" has been echoed by other robopathic killers. Consider the explanation of Lt. Calley in accounting for his personal and indirect killings at My Lai, including his shooting to death of a wounded baby that was attempting to crawl out of a ditch:

> I had tremendous amounts of adrenalin flowing through my body. . . . There was a strong anxiety, I think, that always goes along in situations like that. I was ordered to go in there and destroy the enemy. That was my job on that day. . . . I did not sit down and think in terms of men, women and children. They were all classified the same, and that was the classification that we dealt with—just as enemy soldiers. I felt then, and I still do, that I acted as I was directed, and I carried out the orders that I was given, and I do not feel wrong in doing so. . . .

Lt. Calley was convicted of his crimes, even though the chain of command and guilt up to the incumbent president was legally ignored. In fact, the immediate president, Nixon, saw fit to mitigate Calley's conviction, by releasing him from jail until the appeal was concluded. Perhaps this was done because one robopathic personality, Nixon, can readily understand the acompassionate behavior of another, Calley, to carry out ahuman orders in the line of duty. Additionally, the silent majority of robopathic personalities around the country broke their silence and howled their disapproval of the conviction of one of their people. The robopathic majority apparently found their ideal war hero.

Hardly had the Calley decision been announced when the first of what grew to be 100,000 telegrams of protest were unloaded at the White House in Washington. "Free Calley" resolutions were dropped into the pending baskets of at least nine state legislators. Draft boards quit en masse from Connecticut to New Mexico. Veterans of World War II and Korea tried to surrender to police in several cities for their own war crimes. Among them an ex-marine master sergeant said: "If this man is guilty, he is guilty for the same thing we did. We shot up civilians under orders and killed civilians too." In the city of Calley's verdict, Columbus, Georgia, a

minister preached to a rally crowd gathered in a football
stadium: "There was a crucifixion 2,000 years ago of a man
named Jesus Christ. I don't think we need another crucifixion
of a man named Rusty Calley."

Americans joined together emotionally, if not actively, to
sing one of the most mawkishly constructed but rapidly selling songs (202,000 copies in three weeks) ever written, "The
Battle Hymn of Lt. Calley":

> My name is William Calley,
> I'm a soldier of this land,
> I've vowed to do my duty
> and to gain the upper hand,
> But they've made me out a villain,
> they have stamped me with a brand,
> As we go marching on.

A national poll at the time of Calley's conviction revealed
that about 75 percent of the population disagreed with the
decision. The common theme expressed was that Calley was
"acting under orders." The majority apparently believes that
atrocities within the proper normative social framework are
not deviant, and therefore are not true atrocities.

As often occurs in the case of people who are projected into
the spotlight, there was a retrospective "case history" examination of Lt. Calley's growing-up process. The evidence did
not reveal any spectacular traumas of an abnormal family or
unusual life experiences. Calley was brought up in an average
American family, went to standard schools, and lived in
typical American communities. Lt. Calley was obviously not
a deviant, weirdo, hippie, commie, pinko revolutionary freak.
Perhaps his high school principal summed it up best when he
complimented Calley's behavior in high school: "Rusty was
not brilliant but he did what he was told."

This is the crux of the problem of the robopathic personality. The final product is a standardized personality. A person

who has been shaped to keep his place and follow orders, even when these orders contain the admonition to commit ahuman acts.

THE DEVELOPMENT
OF A ROBOPATHIC PERSONALITY

Before examining the emergence of a robopathic personality it might be well to posit what the robopathic counterpoint personality type might be. One image of this ideal type humanistic personality is what the noted psychologist Abraham Maslow called a *self-actualized* person. Robopaths are at the opposite end of the continuum from this extreme model of a positively socialized, spontaneous, creative, and compassionate person. The self-actualized person according to Maslow has the following characteristics:

1. Clearer, more efficient perception of reality.
2. More openness to experience.
3. An increased integration, wholeness, and unity of the person.
4. Increased spontaneity, expressiveness; full functioning; aliveness.
5. A real self; a firm identity; autonomy; uniqueness.
6. Increased objectivity, detachment, transcendence of self.
7. Recovery of creativeness.
8. Ability to fuse concreteness and abstractness, primary and secondary process cognition, etc.
9. Democratic character structure.
10. Ability to love, etc.

A self-actualized person would have the inner definition and sense of self to resist ahuman robopathic action. "The ability to love" in the true sense would equip this person with a compassion for other people that would deter the kind of atrocious robopathic behavior discussed. All people at birth have the potential for achieving this ideal state of existence and personality.

Fundamentally, the infant begins life with, among others, five basic autonomic physiological drives. It is a sound-making, hunger-driven, defecating, emotional, and sexual animal. Rather rapidly, however, each one of these natural behavioral activities is brought under control and routinized by the culture in which the child is socialized.

The child's utterances are either quietly, in a subtle way, or sharply, dramatically brought under control and channeled. Children begin to learn when they can and cannot make noise, and how making sounds in a certain form and sequence produces remarkable responses in their parents and other people. They determine how they can get nourishment and other needed comforts by acting out certain sounds and postures.

Children rapidly learn that the people around them are often consumed with anxiety about where, when, and how they manage their normal excrements. They later learn that toilet training and words connected with it strangely produce emotional impacts on other children and especially adults.

Children also begin to note that smiles and happy responses produce certain impacts; and crying and tears produce other responses. Children begin to experience pleasure, pain, love, fear, and other emotions.

Sexually, children learn that certain parts of the body have a pleasant tingling effect when stroked or massaged. They also observe that the adults around them are preoccupied (too often in terms of shame) with their own sexual organs, as well as theirs, and that some are very concerned about the public exposure of these parts.

All of these physical, biological, autonomic activities are rather rapidly brought under control and focused by the cultural press. In the extreme, children who learn the "correct responses" within the cultural framework have "adjusted satisfactorily" and receive immediate rewards for their "correct behavior." Such societies produce large numbers of up-tight, conformist, alienated, acompassionate people—who tend to lead a robopathic existence. *In brief, following orders is a heavily rewarded and highly desirable objective in robopathic societies.*

In general, children are more apt to emerge as *robopathic* personalities than *self-actualized* people when their socialization process defines the following interrelated characteristics in the form described.

Ritualism

There is an emphasis on *ritualistic*, heavily prescribed behavior. The child is taught to conform to certain patterns regardless of whether the behavior makes humanistic sense. Dogma and ritualism are heavy patterns imposed on the child. "Do exactly what you are told."

Spontaneity and Creativity

There is limited possibility for the child to act out and develop his or her *spontaneity*. The child is quickly and definitively given precise rules of behavior and its natural spontaneity is crushed. In this onerous process each child has limited opportunity to be *creative* with his or her behavior. The child does not develop the ability to become creative in human relationships and in its general perception of the world. Its perceptions of the surrounding world are precisely programmed and regimented.

Compassion

There is limited or no emphasis in the child's development on caring for others—or on being loving; except in a standardized way, (e.g., "thou shalt"). Also, there are no role-model examples (e.g., parents or other adults) in the child's social configuration who manifest spontaneous, loving, and compassionate behavior. The consequence tends to be an acompassionate robopath.

Self-Righteousness and Image-Involvement

The child learns to maintain an image of correctness at any cost, including the heavy suppression of certain natural tendencies. The child heavily conforms to the highly defined and rigid expectations of its social environment. Conformity enforces this sense of self-righteousness. The child leans toward becoming a superconformist since it is a safer, more heavily approved, and rewarded behavior.

Alienation

Children who conform to all of these conditions tend to experience loneliness and alienation, because in the process of meeting the prescription of the social machines that surround them, they become estranged from their *inner selves*. They have no inner vectors or inner radar. They are socialized to carefully look for cues and conform to the norms that surround them, and perpetuate the image imposed on them from the system. They give up their selves to the social machine. In the process they are alienated not only from themselves but also from others who are isolated in the same way. In their isolated social-boxes they lack the social ability of spontaneity and compassion to relate to other people.

EDUCATING ROBOPATHS

In addition to parents as socializing agents, educational institutions exert a powerful influence on the emergence of robopaths. There is considerable evidence that many educational systems have become social machines that complement robopath-producing families.

Many schools (at all levels) are large, bureaucratic, ahuman teaching machines that place no emphasis on people relating to people. In some cases, actual mechanical teaching machines have replaced human beings in interaction. In other cases, the teachers are as mechanistic in their approach as the machines. As Charles E. Silberman (among many other observers) suggests in his book, *Crisis in the Classroom,* routine, order, and discipline have become more important than humanistic education, and teachers are more concerned with routine and order than education.

In fact, youngsters who display spontaneity are referred to by human teaching machines as "hyperactives." In many cases the normal and healthy exuberance of childhood is viewed as an emotional problem. Increasingly, in many schools around the country, such children who "act out" too much are sedated with various kinds of drugs—to calm them down. These drugs are of course legally administered by the "system." Later, in life, in their teen-age years, when these same young people take drugs outside of the established order, in a kind of self-administered therapy for changing their emotional state, they may be arrested and labeled criminal. The point is that spontaneity is suspect, and is too often placed under rigid controls by a social machine educational system.

One of the social philosophers who envisioned these problems was J. L. Moreno, who in the mid-1920s attempted to develop an innovative "Impromptu School" that would counterattack the educational social machine impact of over-conformity. His rationale was:

> Children are endowed with the gift of spontaneous expression up to the age of 5, while they are still in an unconscious creative state, unhampered by the laws and customs laid down by a long succession of preceding generations. After that they fall heir to accepted methods of expression; they become imitative, turn into automatons and in a large measure are deprived of natural outlets of volitional creation. . . .

Until a certain age all children's learning is spontaneously acquired. . . . Soon, however, the adult
begins to introduce into the child's world subjects unrelated to its needs. The little victim from then on is
pressed by many adult sophistries into learning poems,
lessons, facts, songs and so on, all of which remain
like a foreign substance in an organism. The child
begins to accept as superior that which is taught him
and to distrust his own creative life. So very early in
the life of the individual there is a tendency to mar
and divert creative impulses. . . .

Here the impromptu comes to the rescue. It offers
a school of training which can be practiced in the
small or large group or within the family circle itself.
The impromptu method concerns itself with mental
and emotional states.We do things and learn things
because we are in certain states—states of fear, of love,
of excitement, aspiration, etc. These states may be
directly affected through stimulation and control of
imagination and emotion. When the impromptu in-
structor recognizes the pupil to be lacking in a certain
state, e.g., courage, joy, etc., he places him in a specific
situation in which the lacking state will be empha-
sized. The pupil "plays" that situation, dramatizing
the state impromptu. In other words, if lacking in
courage, he "plays" courage until he learns to be
courageous.

In summary, the "natural" press of socialization by parents,
friends, and school in machine societies often tends to make
children grow into robopathic adults. Many children, however, are able to incorporate the rules, roles, expectations, and
aspirations of the society into their personality and maintain
their spontaneous, creative, and compassionate abilities and
capacities. Children caught in the press of heavy social machine society do not become self-actualized, in the Maslow
sense; they tend to become robopathic role-players and thus
help perpetuate the social machine system.

ROBOPATHOLOGY AND PSYCHOSIS
IN A MACHINE SOCIETY

Robopaths are apt to be "normal" personalities in social machine societies. They are not considered psychotic or mentally ill—even though their compulsive conformity and blank spontaneity often approximate the condition of many people viewed as psychotic. For example, in effect many ritualistic, acompassionate robopaths manifest and parallel the overt appearance of compulsive catatonic schizophrenics, who move around in a ghostlike manner like the "walking dead."

The psychotic syndrome is generally, however, a totally alienated adjustment to the peculiar pressures felt by certain individuals. Under this pressure they unplug from the system and develop an interior world that is for them an insulator against the consensual reality of the larger society they abhor.

Becoming a robopathic personality in a megamachine society is perhaps the easiest; in a sense, it is the most normal adjustment. Maintaining a large measure of spontaneity, creativity, and compassion or love in human interaction places the individual in a "freak role." For example the pure-loving-hippie-flower-child expression of behavior was and is considered by the majority (especially the hippie's parents) bizarre or crazy behavior. Being open in speech; being unashamed of one's body; relating to nature; hugging, touching, feeling, and making love to other people; refusing to serve in the army and kill; and becoming less dependent on machines are generally considered "disturbed behavior" by a society of robopaths. The hippie "freak" experimental human adjustment pattern, that was and is still attempted by millions of young people, has become in terms of the general norm a deviant life style.

The other extreme alternative for disaffiliation or dropping out of an oppressive machine social system is what is commonly referred to as *psychosis*. One simplistic way of viewing psychosis is that in the psychotic role, one evolves a completely unique perception of the world.

Traditionally, many psychotics have assumed roles like God, Joan of Arc, and other classic cultural roles that inherently contain great power. In becoming psychotic and assuming these roles in their fantasies, they have moved from a helpless, oppressed, unhappy position to become supreme beings, often, at least in fantasy, in complete control of the universe. Although these power roles persist in current psychotic syndromes of adjustment, it is interesting to note how other psychotic roles have emerged in megamachine societies.

The noted psychologist Bruno Bettelheim makes the point that the impact of the machine society on contemporary people is so potent that many "psychotic persons end up feeling controlled by mechanical devices that no longer resemble anything human or even animal-like. Thus modern man, when he is haunted, whether sane or profoundly disturbed, is no longer haunted by other men or by grandiose projections of man, but by machines."

Bettelheim describes in detail one spectacular case of the social machine impact on psychopathology in his analytic treatment of "Joey: A 'Mechanical Boy.' " Joey's case is interesting as a parallel to the robopathic syndrome, which may become the conformist psychotic syndrome of the future:

> Joey, when we began our work with him, was a mechanical boy. He functioned as if by remote control, run by machines of his own powerfully creative fantasy. Not only did he himself believe that he was a machine but, more remarkably, he created this impression in others. Even while he performed actions that are intrinsically human, they never appeared to be other than machine-started and executed. On the other hand, when the machine was not working we had to concentrate on recollecting his presence, for

he seemed not to exist. A human body that functions as if it were a machine and a machine that duplicates human functions are equally fascinating and frightening. Perhaps they are so uncanny because they remind us that the human body can operate without a human spirit, that body can exist without soul. And Joey was a child who had been robbed of his humanity. . . . His story has a general relevance to the understanding of emotional development in a machine age.

During Joey's first weeks with us we would watch absorbedly as this at once fragile-looking and imperious nine-year-old went about his mechanical existence. Entering the dining room, for example, he would string an imaginary wire from his "energy source"—an imaginary electric outlet—to the table. There he "insulated" himself with paper napkins and finally plugged himself in. Only then could Joey eat, for he firmly believed that the "current" ran his ingestive apparatus. . . . Many times a day he would turn himself on and shift noisily through a sequence of higher and higher gears until he "exploded," screaming "Crash, crash," and hurling items from his ever present apparatus—radio tubes, light bulbs, even motors or, lacking these, any handy breakable object. (Joey had an astonishing knack for snatching bulbs and tubes unobserved.) As soon as the object thrown had shattered, he would cease his screaming and wild jumping and retire to mute, motionless nonexistence. . . .

"I never knew I was pregnant," his mother said, meaning that she had already excluded Joey from her consciousness. "His birth," she said, "did not make any difference." Joey's father, a rootless draftee in the wartime civilian army, was equally unready for parenthood. So, of course, are many young couples. Fortunately most such parents lose their indifference upon the baby's birth. But not Joey's parents. "I did not want to see or nurse him," his mother declared. "I had

no feeling of actual dislike—I simply didn't want to take care of him." For the first three months of his life Joey "cried most of the time." ...
Joey was convinced that machines were better than people. . . . If he lost or forgot something it merely proved that his brain ought to be thrown away and replaced by machinery. If he spilled something, his arm should be broken and twisted off because it did not work properly. When his head or arm failed to work as it should, he tried to punish it by hitting it. Even Joey's feelings were mechanical. Much later in his therapy, when he had formed a timid attachment to another child and had been rebuffed, Joey cried: "He broke my feelings." ...
Joey had created these machines to run his body and mind because it was too painful to be human. But again and again he became dissatisfied with their failure to meet his need and rebellious at the way they frustrated his will. . . .
So it had been with all other aspects of Joey's existence with his parents. Their reactions to his eating or noneating, sleeping or wakening, urinating or defecating, being dressed or undressed, washed or bathed did not flow from any unitary interest in him, deeply embedded in their personalities. *By treating him mechanically his parents made him a machine.* . . . [Emphasis added.]
One last detail and this fragment of Joey's story has been told. When Joey was 12, he made a float for our Memorial Day parade. It carried the slogan: "Feelings are more important than anything under the sun." Feelings, Joey had learned, are what make for humanity; their absence, for a mechanical existence. With this knowledge Joey entered the human condition.

ROBOPATHS AND SOCIOPATHS

A highly significant and prevalent personality adjustment in a social machine society is to become a *sociopath*. This

personality type has been used interchangeably in the literature with the concept of the psychiatric term psychopath. (I
chose to use the word *sociopath* because it implies a societal
causal context that I believe is more appropriate than a psychological etiology.) The sociopathic personality syndrome
has been rampant in contemporary technocratic societies.
The major characteristic of a sociopath parallels the robopathic personality. The sociopath, like the robopath, lacks
true compassion or empathy for other people. This does not
mean that both personality adjustments do not contain the
capacity or ability to determine or assess the expectations of
other people. It does mean, however, that behavior in both
syndromes is *egocentric*, in the sense that both "empathize"
with others only for selfish purposes.

The concept of the sociopath has been used diversely to
diagnose such historical luminaries as Adolf Hitler, the late
Senator Joseph McCarthy, and many other common, so-
called psychopathic criminal killers. Many people who have
been diagnosed as sociopaths are more perceptively viewed as
arch-robopaths. The use of the robopath concept illuminates
more dimensions of the problem under analysis than the concept of the sociopath. In order to understand the difference
between the two, we should first define more clearly the concept of the sociopath.

The dominant theme of a sociopath is what has varyingly
been called "moral imbecility" or "character disorder." This
type of individual may know "right" from "wrong"—but a
central element of his or her behavior is a lack of any coherent discretionary ability. In brief, the distinction between
right and wrong does not really matter to the sociopath. He
has a moral or character disorder.

Paul Tappan described the sociopath as a person who "has
a condition of psychological abnormality in which there is
neither the overt appearance of psychosis or neurosis, but
there is a chronic abnormal [often illegal] response to the
environment."

Harrison Gough's description further reveals the sociopathic type of personality. A sociopath is "the kind of person who seems insensitive to social demands, who refuses to or cannot cooperate, who is untrustworthy, impulsive, and improvident, who shows poor judgment and shallow emotionality, and who seems unable to appreciate the reactions of others to his behavior."

A basic personality defect of the sociopath is a limited social conscience toward almost all others to whom he relates. A robopath's limited social conscience is less apparent than the sociopath's because his ahuman impact is more obscure and conforming. Arthur Rabin succinctly describes the trait of defective social conscience apparent in the sociopathic personality:

> There are two major related aspects to this notion of defective conscience. . . . The first aspect is represented in the inability . . . to apply the moral standards of society to his behavior; he cheats, lies, steals, does not keep promises, and so on. He has not absorbed the "thou shalts" and the "thou shalt nots" of his society and cultural milieu. The second aspect is that of absence of guilt. Guilt is an important part of any well-developed conscience. When a normal person violates the moral code he feels guilty; he feels unhappy and blames himself for the transgression. . . . Guilt is an unknown experience for the personality with no superego. There is none of this automatic self-punishment that goes along with the commission of immoral and unethical acts. The sociopath continues to behave irresponsibly, untruthfully, insincerely, and antisocially without a shred of shame, remorse, or guilt. He may sometimes express regret and remorse for the actions and crimes which he may have perpetrated; however, these are usually mere words, spoken for the effect, but not really and sincerely felt.

Robopaths and sociopaths are parallel in this regard—neither feels remorse or guilt. A difference is that sociopaths do not usually feel as self-righteous about their destructive acts as robopaths. Cross-compare, for example, the self-righteous pride of a president or an army general who authorizes homicide, with the feigned abject apologies and guilt of a sociopathic killer.

How do humanistic personalities develop in contrast with sociopathic and robopathic personalities? When compared with sociopaths or robopaths, "self-actualized" or humanistic people have adequate and compassionate personalities. Their social selves are developed from consistent patterns of interaction with other people in a humanistic socialization process. The other is usually a parent or some other adequate adult role model from whom the person learns social feelings of *compassion* and *empathy*. Most of the general concepts of empathy and compassion are derived from the works of Charles Horton Cooley, and later developed by J. L. Moreno and G. H. Mead. As Mead developed the theme, "the self arises in conduct when the individual becomes a social object in experience to himself. This takes place when the individual assumes the attitude or uses the gesture which another individual would use and responds to it himself." Through socialization, the child gradually becomes a social being. "The self thus has its origin in communication and in taking the role of the other."

In an analysis that parallels Mead's, Harry Stack Sullivan maintains that the self is made up of "reflected appraisals." Children lack the psychological equipment and experience necessary for rational and clear self-evaluation. The child's self is determined essentially by meaningful children and adults in his world. To the degree that they view him as a good, significant person, to that degree will he conclude that he has value. In reverse, the depreciation of the child by his "significant others'" or socializing agents can provide him with a very negative or low self-image. The cues for his self-definition are transmitted in the form of facial expression, gestures, acts, compliments, and general attitudes. The *positive* cues for self-evaluation are generally not present in the socialization of people who become robopaths.

Many such individuals become sociopaths—like the youths I have described in my book, *The Violent Gang*. To compensate for their negative self-images, they become part of a group in which they can achieve status without responsibility or social-ability. In the violent gang, status is achieved by an act of violence. Persons capable of achieving status in this manner are characteristically acompassionate.

Robopaths are very much like sociopaths in this regard. They do not empathize with "others" in a loving sense. They are too involved with egocentrically conforming to the norms of their social machines to care about the victims of their little or big murders. Conformity or correct behavior supersedes humanistic concerns. For example, *the tragedy of Lt. William Calley is that, like his Nazi death camp robopathic forerunners, he was Everyman in the social machine society "simply doing his job."*

In contrast with robopaths, who are super-conformists, sociopaths are highly impulsive and *unpredictable*. Their actions are unplanned and generally guided by hedonistic whims. This behavior is at the opposite extreme from conforming robopathic behavior.

Sociopaths in dehumanized systems, like robopaths, feel alienated and alone. The sociopath's outrageous and often excessive acts of violence and sex are often efforts on their parts to *feel something*. They carry out excessive acts of violence not to conform but often to validate the fact that they do have emotions and *exist*. For the sociopath, a super-alone and alienated person, to crudely paraphrase Descartes, the theme is "I feel, therefore I exist."

In my study of sociopathic, violent-gang youth, for example, I found that those youths most susceptible to violent-gang membership emerged from a social milieu that trained them inadequately for assuming constructive social roles. The defective socialization process to which they were subjected fostered a lack of social "feelings." At hardly any point were they trained to have human feelings of compassion or responsibility toward another person.

In *The Violent Gang* I noted that the typical sociopathic youth

> tends to be self-involved, exploitative, and disposed toward violent outbursts. This sociopathic type of individual lacks 'social ability' or the ability adequately to assess the role expectations of 'others.' *He is characteristically unable to experience the pain of the violence he may inflict on another, since he does not have the ability to identify or empathize with any others.* The classic sociopathic comment of the King [gang member] who used the bread knife in the assault on Michael Farmer [a gang victim] aptly describes this pattern of feeling: 'What was I thinking about when I did it? Man, are you crazy. I was thinking about whether to do it again!'

This lack of true feeling for others is a characteristic robopathic response. The gang youth will "do it again" to conform to the acompassionate values of his sociopathic violent gang; the robopath will "do it again" to conform to the dictates of an ahuman technological system. This robopathic pattern is exemplified by the corporate entities that *repeatedly* violate various laws designed to protect the environment. Their need for profits is a more significant motivation than the harm inflicted on other people. Again, a notorious example is the "self-involved-exploitative" automobile industry, "violently" attacking the public with its deadly air-pollution machines. In the face of demands for positive change, there is increasing evidence that the industry's robopathic leaders, unconcerned with the devastating impact of their product, are very selfishly concerned with the potential negative effects such changes might have on their financial profits.

Sociopaths can commit the most appalling acts, yet view them without remorse. They have a warped capacity for love. Their emotional relationships, when they exist, are meager, fleeting, and designed to satisfy their own immediate hedonistic desires. Two traits, guiltlessness and lovelessness, conspicuously mark the sociopath as different from other people. These two traits are also characteristic of robopaths. Any robopathic "guilt," however, is vitiated by conformity and the desire for social approval; and their inability to love is fostered by the emphasis on adherence to the norms rather than feeling or concern for others. The robopath, however, like the sociopath, will feign loving emotions in socially appropriate situations.

DIFFERENCES BETWEEN ROBOPATHS
AND SOCIOPATHS

Robopaths are very comparable with sociopaths. Both syndromes involve people who present a veneer of the capacity to love but in effect their behavior is acompassionate and possesses a limited social conscience. Neither type of person feels much remorse or guilt about the ahuman impact of their behavior. Both patterns also "look clean," in the sense that it is difficult to detect the pathology inherent in these two personality types. The robopath's behavior appears to be "cleaner" or "better" than the sociopath's because his behavior is not deviant, in the usual sense of the term.

Robopaths differ from sociopaths in two distinct ways: in terms of their (1) predictability and (2) their deviance.

Robopaths are super-predictable. Their mechanical behavior is seldom erratic. They are, in this regard, "responsible" members of their community. In contrast, the sociopath may and often does erupt at any time.

Robopaths do not "act out" in this unpredictable way. Nor are they deviant from their social context. Their "existence" is validated by the opposite extreme of behavior from the sociopath—they are super-conformists. They are not deviants, because they are the "good" people in the system. They do not receive punishment but rather affirmation. If they are carrying out an ahuman act that has a negative or destructive impact on other people—they are in the same "guiltless position" as the Nazis; their behavior is conformist.

OTHER PERSPECTIVES ON ROBOPATHOLOGY
IN TECHNOCRATIC SOCIETIES

Nazi Germany had many of the hallmarks of a classic robo-pathic society. The leaders and the populace or majority could not really be viewed as sociopaths or psychotics since their behavior was *not deviant* or *unpredictable* in the context of their social system. Yet in spirit and authorized behavior it was one of the most dehumanized social systems in recent history.

Nazi Germany was a technological society characterized by great mechanical achievements. People acting on behalf of the Fatherland were super-self-righteous about their "heroic" acts of production and destruction.

The death camps were manned by highly efficient, self-righteous, guiltless, acompassionate robopaths who compulsively followed orders. They were unlike sociopaths in that their behavior was *predictable* and they had the state's shield of immunity that they were not *deviant*. Hitler's Nazi Germany was the prototype super-efficient technological society of ahuman robopaths.

One of the most comprehensive and fascinating inside reports available on this society of robopaths is Albert Speer's memoir, *Inside the Third Reich*. This remarkable autobiography by Hitler's minister of armaments documents the enormous technological build-up of the system.

In a subtle, significant, and revealing way most of Speer's story deals with the architectural and technical developments of the Third Reich; another part concerns itself with the political intrigue of the robopathic Hitler regime's inner circle. Significantly, there is only a very brief mention of the moral or ahuman qualities of the Nazi regime.

In a most insightful way, a British reporter cogently described Speer in 1944 as the robopath of the future in a technological system:

> Speer is, in a sense, more important for Germany
> today than Hitler, Himmler, Goering, Goebbels, or

the generals. They all have, in a way, become the mere
auxiliaries of the man who actually directs the giant
power machinc—chargcd with drawing from it thc
maximum effort under maximum strain. . . . In him
is the very epitome of the "managerial revolution."
  Speer is not one of the flamboyant and picturesque
Nazis. Whether he has any other than conventional
political opinions at all is unknown. He might have
joined any other political party which gave him a job
and a career. He is very much the successful average
man, well dressed, civil, noncorrupt, very middle-class
in his style of life, with a wife and six children. Much
less than any of the other German leaders does he
stand for anything particularly German or particularly
Nazi. He rather symbolizes a type which is becoming
increasingly important in all belligerent countries: the
pure technician, the classless bright young man without background, with no other original aim than to
make his way in the world and no other means than
his technical and managerial ability. It is the lack of
psychological and spiritual ballast, and the ease with
which he handles the terrifying technical and organizational machinery of our age, which makes this slight
type go extremely far nowadays. . . . This is their age;
the Hitlers and Himmlers we may get rid of, but the
Speers, whatever happens to this particular special
man, will long be with us.

Speer, very much like many sociopathic, homicidal people
I have interviewed, went along with the Hitler's robopathic
gang. Later when caught and convicted, Speer, like many
killer sociopathic gang leaders I knew, expressed his phony
"regrets." (Lt. Calley also expressed some mumbling platitudes of feigned regret about his homicidal behavior.) The
guilt and regrets expressed by Speer somehow do not ring
true.

Robopaths are not, like many sociopaths, lacking in intelligence or in understanding of moral concepts. They are
simply not bound by moral restrictions because they are preoccupied with the technology of their job and with conform-

ing to the dictates of their society. Lt. Calley was very proficient in his technical task of killing a large number of civilians at My Lai. On a more incredible and monumental level, Eichmann, in his administration of the death camps, did a seemingly impossible technical job in systematically overseeing the organized slaughter of over six million people. In the robopath's realm of behavior, technological issues dominate human concerns. In his own way, Speer, as one of the top leaders of the ultimate ahuman technocracy, provides one of the most insightful and devastating commentaries on the potential disaster that might be wrought by future robopathic functionaries in megamachine societies. After twenty years of imprisonment and contemplation in Spandau Prison he concludes:

> Hitler's dictatorship was the first dictatorship of an industrial state in this age of modern technology, a dictatorship which employed to perfection the instruments of technology to dominate its own people. . . . By means of such instruments of technology as the radio and public-address systems, eighty million persons could be made subject to the will of one individual. Telephone, teletype, and radio made it possible to transmit the commands of the highest levels directly to the lowest organs where because of their high authority they were executed uncritically. Thus many offices and squads received their evil commands in this direct manner. The instruments of technology made it possible to maintain a close watch over all citizens and to keep criminal operations shrouded in a high degree of secrecy. To the outsider this state apparatus may look like the seemingly wild tangle of cables in a telephone exchange; but like such an exchange it could be directed by a single will. Dictatorships of the past needed assistants of high quality in the lower ranks of the leadership also—men who could think and act independently. The authoritarian system in the age of technology can do without such men. The means of communication alone enable it

to mechanize the work of the lower leadership. Thus
the type of uncritical receiver of orders is created.

The criminal events of those years were not only an
outgrowth of Hitler's personality. The extent of the
crimes was also due to the fact that Hitler was the first
to be able to employ the implements of technology to
multiply crime.

I thought of the consequences that unrestricted
rule together with the power of technology—making
use of it but also driven by it—might have in the
future. This war ended with remote-controlled rock-
ets, aircraft flying at the speed of sound, atom bombs,
and a prospect of chemical warfare. In five to ten years
it would be possible for an atomic rocket, perhaps
serviced by ten men, to annihilate a million human
beings in the center of New York within seconds. It
would be possible to spread plagues and destroy
harvests. The more technological the world becomes,
the greater is the danger. . . . As the former minister
in charge of a highly developed armaments economy
it is my last duty to state: A new great war will end
with the destruction of human culture and civilization. There is nothing to stop unleashed technology
and science from completing its work of destroying
man which it has so terribly begun in this war. . . .

The nightmare shared by many people that some
day the nations of the world may be dominated by
technology—that nightmare was very nearly made a
reality under Hitler's authoritarian system. Every
country in the world today faces the danger of being
terrorized by technology; but in a modern dictatorship
this seems to me to be unavoidable. Therefore, the
more technological the world becomes, the more essential will be the demand for individual freedom and
the self-awareness of the individual human being as a
counterpoise to technology. . . .

3

SELECTED
OBSERVATIONS
ON TECHNOCRACY
AND
DEHUMANIZATION

Machine-oriented, technocratic societies have produced enormous advantages for people. It would appear that time and space dimensions have been changed for their benefit; leisure time possibilities have increased through automation; the health, wealth, and welfare of many people has apparently been grossly improved by technocratic systems; and this is reflected in a longer life span. Despite these and other apparent gains from modern technology, a chorus of questions and issues have been posed and amplified about the price paid for "technological progress." These central questions and issues may be summarized and included in the following untested (perhaps untestable) propositions:

1. People, in payment for technocratic advantages, have

eroded their natural environment, and ecological doom is imminent.
2. People's coherent self-identities have been fragmented or rendered anonymous by their work roles in a technocratic state.
3. People's relationship to nature, their natural state of existence, and their enjoyment of nature's beauty have been seriously impaired by the over-developed machine society.
4. The dehumanizing aspects of the technocratic system have escalated crime and various forms of alienation on the part of a large segment of the population. This is especially true for young people, and the condition of a megamachine society has produced hostility and misunderstanding between the generations.
5. The technocratic state fosters racism, prejudice, and discrimination, since the subjugation and exploitation of one segment of the population by another is often a natural consequence of an industrialized competitive economic system.
6. The machine society, especially through its exploding mass media, has confused people's sense of *reality* and personal identity. There is a confused blur between mass media news, drama, and live experience. Existence has increasingly become a spectator sport.
7. The technocratic state is largely responsible for the acceleration of various routes of escape from self through drugs, alcohol, mysticism, super-religions, and growing fantasy states of existence.
8. The technocratic state has accelerated the production of ideas, concepts, life styles—in brief, social change occurs to the point where to be aware is to suffer from future shock.
9. The technocratic state has increased both population movements and population concentrations to the point where masses of people are part of a population bomb that is bound to explode.

10. Machines are increasingly grinding out ersatz, synthetic, and planned-obsolescence products to the point where many people have lost the ability to create qualitatively and consumers have abandoned their esthetic tastes for artisanship and artistry. The machine has co-opted human pride in production, a past prime factor in civilization; and it has programmed people to buy the social machine's products not out of need but for "conspicuous consumption."

All of these alleged propositions are true in some measure, and affect people's existential condition. They are central issues that are receiving enormous attention and demand even further analysis and research.

Despite the paucity of direct empirical research, these significant issues about technocracies and their relationship to dehumanization have been analyzed historically in a variety of contexts. Philosophers, theologians, sociologists, and psychologists have labored to understand the various characteristics of this condition. Many profound literary works also deal with the related themes of alienation, bureaucracy, and loneliness in technocratic social systems. This chapter will attempt to review the many theoretical observations that form the foundation for understanding and developing the concept of robopaths in social machines.

The father of many contemporary theories of spontaneous people versus dehumanized machine-people is Dr. J. L. Moreno, the founder of group psychotherapy, sociometry, and psychodrama. In his classic volume *Who Shall Survive?* he contends that humanity's greatest enemy is not the potentially destructive forces of the natural environment, but man as a machine:

> The racial revolution and World War II have divided mankind into several camps, one fighting the other. But the invention of the atomic bomb has given us an excellent didactic lesson of how foolish inter-

human wars are and how unstable and unsafe is the basis of all human existence. We need one another but continue to fight each other. An enemy has appeared on the horizon which is an enemy to all men, which may make an end to all races, superior and inferior, fit or unfit, old and new.

The essence of the problem Moreno poses is that if people become subservient to the machines they produce, they will lose their basic vital creative ability:

> The weakest point in our present day universe is the incapacity of man to meet the machine, the cultural conserve, or the robot, other than through submission.
> First, one may ask how it is possible that a machine-like device can become dangerous to man as a creator. Following the course of man throughout the various stages of our civilization, we find him using the same methods in the making of cultural products which are used later and with less friction by the products of his mind, his technical devices. These methods have always amounted simply to this—*to neglect and abandon the genuine and outstanding creative process in him.*

Moreno points out that people's submission to their machines is a subtle process. The more machines they produce, the more their creative abilities and resources are diminished. People will ultimately become dependent on the precise and effective machines they have produced and lose their fundamental humanistic-creative ability. Moreno warns that unless people face the situation, they may ultimately be defeated:

> The conclusion we can draw from a survey of the position of man as a biological being in the world of today is that thrown into an industrial environment he does not stand up well in the conflict with the machine. The solution of this conflict lies in an heroic measure, not to surrender to the machine, not to halt

its development, but to meet it on even terms and to resort in this battle to resources which are inherent within his organism.

Beyond the controversy, destruction of the unfit or survival of the fit, is a new goal, the survival of a flexible, spontaneous personality make-up, the survival of the creator.

If a fraction of one-thousandth of the energy which mankind has exerted in the conception and development of mechanical devices were to be used for the improvement of our cultural capacity during the moment of creation itself, mankind would enter into a new age of culture, a type of culture which would not have to dread any possible increase of machinery nor robot races of the future. The escape would be made without giving up anything that machine civilization has produced.

Part of the reason for people's preoccupation with creating machines, according to Moreno, is their fear of the unknown. They fear the exigencies of the future and attempt to store up power and patterns of behavior for expected and imminent crises. They do not trust their own spontaneity and creativity —so they package it in a machine, or what he calls a *cultural conserve*. Machines have better memories than people and, in some cases, function more efficiently; consequently, more and more people become more and more dependent on machines as cultural conserves. Moreno warns that people in this process ultimately lose their spontaneity and creativity ability—the *primary* resource of being human:

As our perfectionism has failed us again and again in its application to us as biological and social beings, as individuals and as a society of individuals, we give up hope and invest it in zoomatons. The pathological consequences are enormous. Man turns more and more into a function of cultural and technological conserves, puts a premium on power and efficiency and loses credence in spontaneity and creativity.

The transaction of trading humanistic values for machine benefits is a theme that runs through considerable literature. Selling one's soul for a "mess of pottage" or a Faustian deal with the devil has some parallels with trading human spontaneity, creativity, and people's relationships with nature for the immediate gratifications of a *social machine*—an entity that on the surface appears to provide a measure of security but is one that may ultimately control and enslave its creator and master. One clear end result is the enslavement of people in robopathic roles in bureaucratic machines.

In a vein similar to Moreno's brilliant analysis, Lewis Mumford wrote in *The Transformations of Man* and in his later works about people's increasing mechanization and subservience to machines: "Modern man has already depersonalized himself so effectively that he is no longer man enough to stand up to his machines. . . . Automaton man will become completely alienated from his world and reduced to nullity—the kingdom and the power and the glory now belong to the machine."

Such enslavement to machines is perceptively portrayed by Charlie Chaplin in *Modern Times*. The film's hero works on an assembly line turning a bolt with a wrench in the same motion all day long. Later, his body compulsively moves to the rhythm of the machine all the way home from work. Even at home while he is eating dinner his head and body jerk to the beat of the machine.

Lewis Mumford has also described the way in which time regulates the lives of people in the social machine:

> The first characteristic of modern machine civilization is its temporal regularity. From the moment of waking, the rhythm of the day is punctuated by the clock. Irrespective of strain or fatigue, despite reluctance or apathy, the household rises close to its set hour. Tardiness in rising is penalized by extra haste in eating breakfast or in walking to catch the train: in the long run, it may even mean the loss of a job or of advancement in business. Breakfast, lunch, dinner,

occur at regular hours and are of definitely limited duration: a million people perform these functions within a very narrow band of time, and only minor provisions are made for those who would have food outside this regular schedule. As the scale of industrial organization grows, the punctuality and regularity of the mechanical regime tend to increase with it: the timeclock enters automatically to regulate the entrance and exit of the worker, while an irregular worker—tempted by the trout in spring streams or ducks on salt meadows—finds that these impulses are as unfavorably treated as habitual drunkenness. . . .

The existence of a machine civilization, completely timed and scheduled and regulated, does not necessarily guarantee maximum efficiency in any sense. Time-keeping establishes a useful point of reference, and is invaluable for co-ordinating diverse groups and functions which lack any other common frame of activity. In the practice of an individual's vocation such regularity may greatly assist concentration and economize effort. But to make it arbitrarily rule over human functions is to reduce existence itself to mere time-serving and to spread the shades of the prison house over too large an area of human conduct.

In his classic analysis of the city, sociologist Georg Simmel echoes and reinforces Mumford's time thesis:

Punctuality, calculability, exactness are forced upon life by the complexity and extension of metropolitan existence and are not only most intimately connected with its money economy and intellectualistic character. These traits must also color the content of life and favor the exclusion of those irrational, instinctive, sovereign traits and impulses which aim at determining the mode of life from within, instead of receiving the general and precisely schematized form of life from without.

Dostoevsky railed against the precise machine society and its exclusion of "irrational, instinctive and sovereign traits."

The possible problems of a clear, exact, and "rational" society
are poetically assessed by Dostoevsky in his *Notes from
Underground*:

> Then—this is all what you say—new economic
> relations will be established, all ready-made and
> worked out with mathematical exactitude, so that
> every possible question will vanish in the twinkling
> of an eye, simply because every possible answer to it
> will be provided. Then the "Palace of Crystal" will
> be built. Then . . . In fact, those will be halcyon days.
> Of course there is no guaranteeing . . . that it will not
> be, for instance, frightfully dull then (for what will
> one have to do when everything will be calculated and
> tabulated?), but on the other hand everything will
> be extraordinarily rational. Of course boredom may
> lead you to anything. It is boredom sets one sticking
> golden pins into people, but all that would not mat-
> ter. [This notion was apparently derived from an al-
> leged practice of Cleopatra, who supposedly stuck
> gold pins into the nipples of slave girls to relieve her
> boredom.] What is bad . . . is that I dare say people
> will be thankful for the gold pins then. Man is stupid,
> you know, phenomenally stupid; or rather he is not
> at all stupid, but he is so ungrateful that you could not
> find another like him in all creation. I, for instance,
> would not be in the least surprised if all of a sudden,
> apropos of nothing, in the midst of general prosperity
> a gentleman with an ignoble, or rather with a reaction-
> ary and ironical, countenance were to arise and put-
> ting his arms akimbo, say to us all: "I say, gentlemen,
> hadn't we better kick over the whole show and scatter
> rationalism to the winds, simply to send these loga-
> rithms to the devil, and to enable us to live once more
> at our own sweet foolish will!"

The crystal palace of a "rational" society includes the absurd acquisition of material goods for ostentatious display
rather than for use. Without any real concern for their own
human needs, the needs of others, or the depletion of natural

resources, people in technocratic systems get caught up in acquiring material goods to signify status and affluence. In fact, the ritual of "shopping" for dysfunctional status objects has become a dominant mass activity for bored people.

One of the patterns of materialism involves the acquisition of prettily packaged people, rather than inanimate products, for display purposes. The handsome high school football hero and the pert, pug-nosed blonde are the ideal "human packages" traditionally sought after by teen-agers. In later life these same other-directed people, who are robopathic in their orientation, seek out the correct human package to help fulfill the correct image required for advancement in their occupational roles. In brief, people appear to have become more concerned with the images of people and things than with their function in serving human needs.

In this same fashion people have invented and used a variety of mechanical contraptions and devices that look useful but in fact may be dysfunctional, in overview. Consider certain aspects of transportation. People are carried cross-country in a remarkably short period of time—less than five hours for a coast-to-coast trip of 3,000 miles. These same people, arrived at their destination, then find themselves in the absurd position of having to spend another five hours traveling the twenty-five or fifty miles from the airport to the city.

In New York—a world-wide symbol of machine devastation —the absurd trip from the airport to the downtown air terminal is almost impossible during certain hours of the day. Even more incredible is the trip from the air terminal to a hotel. Transportation "progress" here involves a situation so absurd that traveling on foot is far superior to the total machine conglomerate of taxis, subways, or buses.

In many situations of modern technocratic transportation the only solution is the facetious remark that has almost become a truism: "You can't get there from here." (Try to go from the east side to the west side of Manhattan; or even worse, go anywhere on a Los Angeles "freeway.")

The final product of the machine impact has commanded

the attention of many other social philosophers. In a perceptive diatribe, sociologist Ernest van den Haag examines the
destruction of people's personal identities:

> In a material sense, the assembly-line shaping,
> packaging and distributing of persons, of life, occurs
> already. Most people perch unsteadily in mass-pro-
> duced, impermanent dwellings throughout their lives.
> They are born in hospitals, fed in cafeterias, married
> in hotels. After terminal care, they die in hospitals,
> are shelved briefly in funeral homes, and are finally
> incinerated.
>   On each of these occasions—and how many others?
> —efficiency and economy are obtained and individual-
> ity and continuity stripped off. If one lives and dies
> discontinuously and promiscuously in anonymous sur-
> roundings, it becomes hard to identify with anything,
> even one's own individuality. The rhythm of individ-
> ual life loses autonomy, spontaneity, and distinction
> when it is tied into a stream of traffic and carried along
> according to the speed of the road, as we are, in going
> to work, or play, or in doing anything. Traffic lights
> signal when to stop and go, and much as we seem
> to be driving we are driven. To stop spontaneously,
> to exclaim, Verweile doch Du bist so schoen (Stay,
> for you are beautiful), may not lose the modern Faust
> his soul—but it will cause a traffic jam.

Van den Haag postulates in this context that one possible
motive for delinquency is that it is "a way of getting out of
line." He further comments: "Crime, by its ultimate irration-
ality, may protest against the subordination of individual
spontaneity to social efficiency."

Several reaction formations to anonymity or loss of identity
may be noted. People develop histrionic qualities. They impersonate, get a name—better a pseudonym than to remain
nameless; better a borrowed character than none; better to
impersonate than never to feel like a person. In brief, people

powerfully attempt to obtain and perpetuate an *image.* People also attempt to become "interesting" (no doubt unconsciously to become interested) by buying ready-made individuality, through "sending for," "enrolling in," or "reading up on" something, or "going places." People with a limited sense of self try hard and pay heavily to be very "in." They will, *whether they like it or not,* read the "in" books, go to "in" movies, and buy "in" clothes. The intrinsic function and enjoyment of a behavioral act is secondary to the *image* that is fostered and presented.

This surrealistic version of the mass impact of media on human identity has already come to pass. People, young and old, through T.V., radio employee bulletins, newspapers and advertising, have their personalities and viewpoints formulated and shaped at every turn. Mass media instructions are now explicit determinants of, among other areas of behavior, how, where, and with whom it is best to have sex; the exact clothes to wear on all occasions; how and in what way children and parents, and husbands and wives, should relate; and the right candidate who deserves the vote. Very little, if anything, is left to anyone's personal imagination.

Even in this regard, people's personal imaginations are defined by the increasing bombardment from all directions on the right fantasies. Not even these scenes are private territory. No wonder many young people have tuned in and turned on to drugs that provide an extreme retreat from the mass media onslaught. The drugs produce an instant, if only transitory, sense of being human. Many young people will risk almost any peril, including addiction, to retrieve their state of consciousness from the mass impact. They will take any chance to—in their own words—"do their own thing."

Robert K. Merton describes the effect the mass media have on their audiences:

> They feel themselves the object of manipulation. They see themselves as the target for ingenious meth-

ods of control, through advertising which cajoles, promises, terrorizes; through propaganda that, utilizing available techniques, guides the unwitting audience into opinions which may or may not coincide with the best interests of themselves or their affiliates; through cumulatively subtle methods of salesmanship which may simulate values common to both salesman and client for private and self-interested motives. In place of a sense of *Gemeinschaft*—genuine community of values—there intrudes *pseudo-Gemeinschaft*—the feigning of personal concern with the other fellow in order to manipulate him better.

In this same area of technocracy in a mass society, according to sociologist C. Wright Mills, mass media determine people's identities, aspirations, techniques of "success," and notions of how to feel and how to escape. The mass media tell people (1) who they are—*identity*; (2) they tell them what they want to be—*aspirations*; (3) they tell them how to succeed —*techniques*; and (4) finally, the media tell people how to feel when they are that way even when they are not—*escape*.

The mass media formula is not attuned to the development of humanism. It is a formula of a pseudo-world that the media have invented and sustained. Mills asserts that the structural trends of mass society and the manipulative character of its technocratic communication technique segregate people into routines and boxes. In smaller communities people know each other more fully, because they meet in many aspects of the total life routine. The members of masses in a metropolitan society know one another only as fractions in a specialized milieu: the man who fixes the car, the girl who serves lunch, the saleslady, the women who take care of one's child at school during the day. Mills notes that prejudgment and stereotype flourish when people meet in such ways. The range of humanistic qualities does not emerge in the fragmentary situations of social machine societies.

People stuck in their routines do not transcend, even by

discussion, much less by action, their compartmentalized lives. They do not gain a view of the overall structure of their society and of their roles within it. The city-machine, for example, is a structure composed of sub-environments. People thus tend to be separated and alienated from one another. Mills cogently observes:

> The "stimulating variety" of the city does not stimulate the men and women of "the bedroom belt," the one-class suburbs, who can go through life knowing only their own kind. If they do reach for one another, they do so only through stereotypes and prejudiced images of the creatures of other milieux. Each is trapped by his confining circle; each is cut off from easily identifiable groups. It is for people in such narrow milieux that the mass media can create a pseudo-world within themselves as well.

In technocratic societies, in every major area of life, the loss of a sense of structure and the submergence of identity into a powerless milieu is a dominant fact. In the political order men cannot see the totality, cannot see the top, and cannot state the issues that will, in fact, determine the whole structure in which they live and their place within it. This partially accounts for the doomsday and the automated battlefield developments. People become powerless.

BUREAUCRACY
AS A SOCIAL MACHINE

The subjugation of people in the social machine of bureaucracy deserves extensive attention since it is an important theme that underlies the concept of robopathic behavior and is the foundation for many problems of mass societies. Bureaucracy is an ultimate system wherein people's humanism is consciously reduced to a minimum level. Human emotions and expressions are antithetical to the smooth functioning of a bureaucratic social machine. Bureaucracy is a significant category of the larger scheme of robopathology.

In a bureaucratic organization the typical participant occupies an "office" or a position in a hierarchy. In people's actions associated with their status, in the hierarchy, people issue orders to other people. Everyone is subject to impersonal orders, and action is oriented to the impersonal machine system.

People obey authority and laws not as people but in their capacity as robopaths in a corporate system. The only human interaction that takes place in a total bureaucracy takes place in terms of the *demands of the office*. People in a bureaucratic social machine do not give or take orders as people, but only as "statuses" or as positions in an impersonal, ordered *social machine*.

In the bureaucratic organization of offices the principle of a hierarchy is significant. Each lower office is under the control and supervision of a higher one. There is limited individual or personal power. The power flows from the position, not from the human occupant of the role.

Only people who have demonstrated an adequate technical training are qualified to be members of the administrative staff of a (bureaucratically) organized group, and only such persons are eligible for appointment to official positions.

The role played by technical competence in bureaucracy is significant and emanates from the pervasive concern that is given to the rational pursuit of the ends of the organization. If an organization is to attain its goals, it is paramount that its personnel be as efficient and as competent as possible.

Their efficiency is dependent on the extent to which they possess technical competence. A consequence of this emphasis is that people are selected on the basis of impersonal examinations rather than according to any humanistic characteristics. People in large social machine organizations are therefore only ciphers in a vast machine. The status-occupants' value to the organization has nothing to do with the fact that they are human. In fact, if they were robots, devoid of any feelings (other than those related to technical competence), they would be ideal and more valuable to the machine.

In a bureaucracy administrative acts, decisions, and rules are recorded in writing even in cases where oral discussion is the rule or is even mandatory. Written materials and files assume more importance than human interaction. Over the long haul of being a part of the bureaucratic entity, an individual's interpersonal (human) skills defer and take a back seat to one's performance *"on record."* Not only does the bureaucratic social machine record actions taken and the resulting consequences; it also records policies formed, and carefully preserves the rules and regulations which give form to the system. All of this constitutes the "file." People are the raw material that feeds the file and *paper* very often becomes more important than people. In this context the burning of draft cards by young people is among other dimensions of protest a symbolic act of destroying their paper existence.

The processes of filing and paperwork in the bureaucracy are sardonically described by a stereotyped classic advertising executive in a movie called *Joe*:

> You see those buildings, Joe? . . . those beautiful monuments of concrete and glass? I work in one of them. You know what they do in those buildings, Joe? They move paper. They move paper. That's right. They pick it up in one place and move it to another place. They pass it all around their offices. And the more paper you move, the more important you are. The more important you are, the more they pay you. And if you want to show how really important you are, you know what you can get away with? You make little paper airplanes and you sail them right up somebody else's ass.

One major humanistic problem with bureaucracy as a *social machine* is the displacment of goals. People become so ritualistic in "moving paper around" that they forget the human needs that are supposed to be filled by the social machine's goals.

In this context Merton comments on the bureaucratic expert: "An extreme product of this process of displacement of goals is the bureaucratic virtuoso, who never forgets a single rule binding his action and hence is unable to assist many of his clients."

Anyone who has attempted to avail himself of the services of modern mass medical treatment is well aware of how the bureaucratic social machine can eliminate the potential help that might have been provided by the medical "bureaucratic virtuoso," who has become a classic robopath. If a *patient* (not a person) appears at the wrong time, is of the wrong sex, age, or skin color (blacks are not treated by certain hospitals in the South), or has the wrong affliction, that patient can suffer or even die before he or she is treated by the robopaths who operate the bureaucratic hospital social machines.

The actual case of a child who was badly burned reveals the senseless inflexibility of robopaths to act humanistically within a hospital machine:

BADLY BURNED BABY
FINALLY GIVEN HELP

An 11-month-old Palms boy is in critical condition today at County-USC Medical Center after he suffered first- and second-degree burns in a bathtub Saturday. According to police reports the child was taken to two hospitals—Southern California X Hospital and X Medical Center—before he finally was treated for the burns at County-USC Medical Center. [The hospital's actual name is replaced by an X, since its administrators have subsequently adopted a more humanistic policy in dealing with such emergencies.] Police said Sean Hurley, 3661½ Westwood Blvd., was left in a bathtub by a baby-sitter about 7 p.m. Saturday. The baby-sitter told police the water was running into the tub, but it was not hot. She reportedly left the child in the tub with the water running and went into another room. Then she heard the baby scream. She told police she found the baby in the bath with the hot water running. She said she quickly took him to Southern California X Hospital, accompanied by the child's mother, Darlene Hurley, of the Westwood Blvd. address. Mrs. Hurley was out at the time of the accident. The X Hospital apparently told the baby-sitter it had no facilities for treating the burns, according to the police report. Officials there advised the baby-sitter to go to X Medical Center. Again—according to the police report—the woman said she was told there were no facilities for treating the burns at X [Medical Center] and that she was told to take the child to the County-USC facility. A spokesman at the Southern California X Hospital said today the child was given treatment for relief of pain and other preventive measures were taken to keep the burns from worsening. He said they have no facilities for treating burns. For this reason it was recommended the child be taken to X Medical Center, he said. Officials at the X Medical Center could not be reached for comment this morning.

This type of bureaucratic horror story is more or less repeated daily in "humane hospitals" around the world, because robopaths treat people as objects rather than as humans. The humanistic goals of organizations become obfuscated by the complexity of the ahuman system.

Bureaucratic inadequacies in orientation involve a built-in incapacity that clearly derives from the normal structural conditions of certain social machines. Merton describes the process as follows: "(1) An effective bureaucracy demands reliability of response and strict devotion to regulations. (2) Such devotion to the rules leads to their transformation to absolutes; they are no longer conceived as relative to a set of purposes. (3) This interferes with ready adaptation under special conditions not clearly envisaged by those who drew up the general rules. (4) Thus, the very elements which conduce toward efficiency in general produce inefficiency in specific instances." This occurs when the people in the system become mindless robopaths following rules rather than being concerned with people in human interaction. The rules they follow are no longer functional. They become useless symbols of the mass dehumanized organization.

Another facet in the manufacture of robopaths in bureaucracies is related to the fact that the bureaucrats' official lives are planned in terms of graded careers. They are rewarded by such organizational devices as "promotion by seniority, pensions, and incremental salaries [in order] to provide incentives for disciplined action and conformity to the official regulations. The official is tacitly expected to and largely does adapt his thoughts, feelings, and actions to the prospect of this career." A robopath must conform in order to move up in the hierarchy.

Paradoxically, the very devices which increase conformity lead to a concern with strict adherence to regulations. This path of action induces timidity and conservatism. It also veers toward a displacement of sentiments from human goals onto mechanical means, and fosters a tremendous symbolic significance of the means (rules). Bureaucrats are thus trained toward becoming unsentimental actors in a vast empire of symbols and definitions. In the process they lose contact with human needs and become robopaths.

One bureaucratic role-occupant dismally views his situation from the inside in the following poignant and pertinent portrayal of his robopathic state of existence:

> This way to the palace. Point your car along a winding drive-way up the green hillside shaded with great elm trees. Enter the wide and friendly doorway and look at the murals in our lobby. They will tell you the story of our industry. As you go through the offices, you will probably marvel as we did at all the comforts and services we have. Imagine a sea of blond desks with tan chairs, outdoor lighting pouring in everywhere, roomy offices with individually-controlled air-conditioning and area-controlled Music by Muzak

coming out of the walls. We need few private secre-
taries. All we have to do is pick up a phoning device
and dictate our message to a disc that whirls in a
sunny room in another part of the building. Here a
pool of stenographers type all day long with buttons
in their ears. We don't see them and they don't see
us, but they know our voices.

A high-speed pneumatic tube system winds through
the entire building. We send material from one office
to another not by messenger but by torpedo containers
traveling twenty-five feet a second. Simply have the at-
tendant put your paper, magazine, or memo in the
plastic carrier. He inserts the container in the tube,
dials the appropriate number, and, whoosh, it is shot
across the building.

There is a complete sound system throughout
headquarters. If, for example, a bad storm is forecast,
there will be an "Attention Please," and you may go
home early. At noon, enjoy movies in an auditorium
the size of a small theater, visit the library, watch the
World Series on color TV, or play darts and table
tennis in the game room. The finest catering service
and a staff of friendly waitresses bring you luncheon.
Then go to the company store, pitch horseshoes, or
take a brief stroll under the elms. . . .

I sometimes have a feeling of being in limbo.
More than ever one feels—ungratefully—over-pro-
tected. While on the job, I actually can't feel hot or
cold. I can't even get sick. This will sound ridiculous,
but when the company obtained a supply of influenza
shots, I found myself in the absurd position of refusing
one. For some reason I wanted a chance to resist the
flu in my own way.

This description of life in the crystal palace is a modern
version of Kafka. In his classic novel *The Trial*, Kafka poetically and symbolically describes the plight of another individual caught in the bureaucratic web of a *social machine*. In
The Trial, Joseph K., a minor bureaucrat who works as a

bank clerk, is arrested, released, and generally harassed by the
State. He can never find out why he has been arrested:

> "You can't go out, you are arrested." "So it seems,"
> said K. "But what for?" he added. "We are not au-
> thorized to tell you that. Go to your room and wait
> there. Proceedings have been instituted against you,
> and you will be informed of everything in due course.
> I am exceeding my instructions in speaking freely to
> you like this. But I hope nobody hears me except
> Franz, and he himself has been too free with you,
> against his expressed instructions. If you continue to
> have as good luck as you have had in the choice of
> your warders, then you can be confident of the final
> result." K. felt he must sit down, but now he saw that
> there was no seat in the whole room except the chair
> beside the window. . . .
>   Who could these men be? What were they talking
> about? What authority could they represent? K. lived
> in a country with a legal constitution, there was uni-
> versal peace, all the laws were in force; who dared
> seize him in his own dwelling? . . .
>   Without wishing it K. found himself decoyed into
> an exchange of speaking looks with Franz, none the
> less he tapped his papers and repeated: "Here are my
> identification papers." "What are your papers to us?"
> cried the tall warder. "You're behaving worse than a
> child. What are you after? Do you think you'll bring
> this fine case of yours to a speedier end by wrangling
> with us, your warders, over papers and warrants? We
> are humble subordinates who can scarcely find our way
> through a legal document and have nothing to do with
> your case except to stand guard over you for ten hours
> a day and draw our pay for it. That's all we are, but
> we're quite capable of grasping the fact that the high
> authorities we serve, before they would order such an
> arrest as this, must be quite well informed about the
> reasons for the arrest and the person of the prisoner.
> There can be no mistake about that. Our officials,
> so far as I know them, and I know only the lowest
> grades among them, never go hunting for crime in the

populace, but, as the Law decrees, are drawn toward the guilty and must then send out us warders. That is the Law. How could there be a mistake in that?"

The charade between Joseph K. and various robopaths—who always claim that "we are only doing our duty"—goes on interminably throughout the story in K.'s bedroom, at his job, wherever he goes.

One inference that can be drawn from this allegory is that K. is the everyman-rat caught in the maze of the social machine's bureaucratic maze. The trial and the offense may be poetically related to the fact that K. has helped to create his own destiny—since he is in part responsible for the bureaucratic system that is now strangling him. He helped the people machine emerge, perpetuated it, and now (like many of us) must pay the price of capitulation to its outrageous demands and devastating atrocities. Part of the toll paid is a condition of powerlessness and alienation.

ALIENATION
AND SOCIAL MACHINES

People "involved" with and subjugated by social machines tend to have a sense of *personal* disassociation from human groups and their society. They tend to feel disaffiliated and apart. In brief, they have a sense of alienation.

People in modern industrial societies have rapidly become detached from nature, from their old gods, from the technology that has transformed their environment and now threatens to destroy it. Work and its product are no longer meaningful or fulfilling. In the social machines of a technocratic society, people are alienated and are adrift in a world that has little meaning for them and over which they exercise limited power. They become strangers to themselves and to others. On this overall theme Erich Fromm comments: "Alienation as we find it in modern society is almost total; it pervades the relationship of man to his work, to the things he consumes, to his fellows, and to himself."

In a technocratic society people have an indefinable sense of loss; a sense that their lives have become impoverished. Their alienation fundamentally involves a separation from their natural environment and from their selves.

In regard to people's break with nature, Susanne Langer cogently writes in her book, *Philosophy in a New Key:*

> We have put many stages of artifice and device, of manufacture and alteration, between ourselves and the rest of nature. The ordinary city-dweller knows nothing of the earth's productivity; he does not know the sunrise and rarely notices when the sun sets; ask him in what phase the moon is, or when the tide in the harbor is high, or even how high the average tide runs, and likely as not he cannot answer you. Seed-time and harvest are nothing to him. If he has never witnessed an earthquake, a great flood, or a hurricane, he probably does not feel the power of nature as a reality surrounding his life at all. . . . Nature, as man has always known it, he knows no more.

The development of the hippie counterculture phenom-enon may be partially viewed in this context. Communes in-volve an extremist effort at an idyllic return to the land and the nature environment. One young leader, when pushed to define the major conditions of the movement, commented: "Basically we want to work out a different relationship to the land than the plastic society. We want to return to nature."

This goal is a lofty and almost necessary one for a mega-machine society that has become alienated from nature by choking the land with overpopulated cities and concrete highways; that has overused the general land; and that has with the same impact filled the air and water with pollution. Many dropped-out young people dream about and have at-tempted to return to the tribal position of the American Indian; or to the more satisfying life of a more closely-knit extended family—a situation where adults and children can live more intimately and humanely in a cohesive, face-to-face, primary group. The goal, therefore, is a more cohesive, emotionally closer, fundamentally human unit living in a less alienated, more natural state.

The view that people in machine societies have moved too far away from each other and the basic quality of their natural environment may also be felt (perhaps not as acutely) by other segments of the population. The middle-class suburban family finally moving into their "garden apartment"-type house with a 9' x 9' plot of plastic green yard where they barbecue neatly butchered meat on a chromium-plated electrified barbecue machine may in a more tortured fashion than the commune dwellers be attempting to reach back into history toward a simpler, more natural life.

Theodore Roszak, in his book *The Making of a Counter Culture*, describes a similar theme and process at work. For Roszak, the counterculture of the young is

> the matrix in which an alternative, but still excessively fragile future is taking shape. Granted that alternative comes dressed in a garish motley, its costume borrowed from many and exotic sources—from depth psychiatry, from the mellowed remnants of left-wing ideology, from the oriental religions, from Romantic *Weltschmerz*, from anarchist social theory, from Dada and American Indian lore, and, I suppose, the perennial wisdom. Still it looks to me like all we have to hold against the final consolidation of a technocratic totalitarianism in which we shall find ourselves ingeniously adapted to an existence wholly estranged from every thing that has ever made the life of man an interesting adventure.

BASIC ELEMENTS OF ALIENATION
AND ROBOPATHOLOGY

The impact of alienation on people in groups has been cogently summarized by many sociologists, especially Melvin

Seeman. There are five fundamental usages or meanings that identify the concept of alienation: (1) powerlessness, (2) meaninglessness, (3) normlessness, (4) isolation, and (5) self-estrangement. These usages will be analyzed, in turn, as they relate to the concept of robopaths.

Powerlessness

People in technocratic systems are lost in a maze of machines, regulations, and complex rules. They tend to be powerless to control the many variables that affect their lives in a machine-dominated society. This condition fosters the alienation of people from other people and the degradation of humans into commodities and helpless pawns. The proliferation and growth of bureaucratic social machines thus enlarges the condition of powerlessness as a characteristic of the robopathic existence.

The notion of powerlessness has a significant meaning in contemporary societies. People seem to be increasingly powerless in their ability to do anything meaningful about certain major problems. They appear to be more and more out of touch or powerless to control the forces of air pollution, war, and other negative dimensions of their lives.

The enormous development and impact of mass media machines have also had a considerable impact. People's sense of powerlessness partially relates to the size and intensity of issues that come within the scope of their awareness and the relative control they have over these issues. As people are increasingly made aware, through mass media (in particular, T.V.), of such enormous issues as war, famine, crime, and injustice, their *felt* sense of *powerlessness* and alienation grows. This occurs because of the growing gap between their limited control and the size of the problem.

People working in industrial complexes are especially locked into their own unique boxes of powerlessness. In their bureaucratic stalls they are relatively powerless to do anything about the manifest problems that surround them. They are re-

luctant to rock any boats because they are lulled into a tranquil
state of acceptance by the system.

(Recently I addressed the heads of various departments
—social welfare, probation, personnel, etc.—of one of the
largest counties in the country on the theme of the machine
society and bureaucracy. All honorable men, they acknowl-
edged that they were in a bureaucratic "box" that no longer
permitted them the possibility of any logical or sensible action
on the social problems they were supposed to solve. Locked in
their social machines of sterility, they tranquilized themselves
and could only rationalize their predicament by saying, as one
executive did, "We've painted ourselves into an important
corner. We can't do anything anymore but wait until re-
tirement.")

Meaninglessness

People tend to feel meaningless when they attempt to
confront the large maze of objects they encounter each day
in a mass technocratic society. A simple drive on a crowded
freeway is sufficient to give a person a sense of personal meaninglessness. The assembly-line approach to health care in
most modern (almost automated) hospitals also underlines
this contemporary condition. In some measure Alvin Toffler's
theme in his book *Future Shock* illuminates this point. Individuals are inundated with events and facts to the point where
their sense of priority and their personal meaning are grossly
diminished. They have, he asserts, lost a considerable amount
of their power to control their future destiny.

People participating in social machines are grossly aware of
their personal meaninglessnesses. They are reduced to a robopathic status where their behavior is controlled by the established ritualistic definitions of the machine in which they
function.

A pertinent analysis of the prototype executive in America
is Arthur Miller's classic salesman, Willy Loman. Willy
eventually commits suicide when the meaninglessness of his

life becomes apparent. Throughout his sociodrama Willy refuses to accept the fact that he is simply a part of the machine—and that as he wore out like his (planned obsolescent) refrigerator, he was no longer of any value or meaning simply because he was a *human* being. In his preoccupation with his job and his aspirations, Willy alienates his sons, who both leave home. Toward the end of the drama, they return home from their aimless wanderings to find their father being ground under by his feelings of irrelevance. The mother pleads to her sons (and the world): "Attention must be paid —a man is dying." At the end of the road emotionally and spiritually, Willy concludes that his life is now meaningless and all he is worth to his family is the value of his paper insurance policy. He concludes toward the end of the play, "You end up worth more dead than alive."

As depicted in *Death of a Salesman*, the value of people compared to machines is increasingly diminished and meaningless. The meaninglessness of people compared to machines is further illustrated, for example, in the following news report:

PLANT SHUT DOWN:
APCD SAYS DUST WAS MARRING CARS

Air pollution officials shut down a South Gate chemical plant Tuesday for emitting a chemical into the air that they said has damaged thousands of automobiles and homes in South Gate, Cudahy and Bell Gardens.

An Air Pollution Control District spokesman said [the company] was cited last week for the infraction and that a complaint will be filed with the district attorney this week. . . .

The chemical, anhydrous sodium metasilicate, is a light powdery substance which floats freely in the air but after making contact with a hot surface, such as a car, melts and sticks to the object.

Residents in the area claim that after the white

chemical is removed it leaves a pit on metal surfaces and windows

Officials said the chemical, which is used to make cleaning fluids, is a corrosive and can cause serious damage to metal and glass.

The destruction of car surfaces produced an immediate shutdown of the plant. On the other hand, the issue of this factory's and countless other factories' destructive impact on human body tissue (particularly the lungs) does not seem to trigger any real governmental action.

The ultimate devaluation and meaninglessness of people compared to machines may be found in a report by the U. S. government concerning experiments with "death rays" and neutron bombs. Officials *proudly* reported their success with the ultimate weapon: "A soldier in a tank or an office staff in a building would die, but the tank and the building would remain intact."

Normlessness

Emile Durkheim first presented the concept of *anomie* to account for the presence of deviance in society. In its elemental sense, anomie means normlessness, or a situation where individual behavior is no longer properly controlled by the society.

The concept of anomie deserves special attention in the examination of the overall condition of alienation in social machine societies. The concept was first presented by Durkheim to illuminate the manner in which the norms of a society become useless in controlling people's behavior.

The concept of anomie has been used by many sociological researchers and theorists to attempt to account for the problems of deviance. Robert K. Merton deals with anomie as a situation where there is a "breakdown in the cultural structure, occurring particularly when there is an acute disjunction between the cultural norms and goals and the . . . capacities of members of the group to act in accord with them."

Problems of deviance arise when people cannot achieve the cultural goals through the available means. They then attempt to succeed by any means necessary, and this generally includes deviant, alienated behavior.

Whereas Durkheim and Merton dealt with overall societies in terms of normlessness, Erving Goffman examined the arena of simple interaction or conversation, as it relates to normlessness. In a provocative article, "Alienation from Interaction," Erving Goffman focuses on the manner in which normlessness or alienation can occur between people in everyday situations. For example, according to Goffman, this condition can obtain in the simplest conversation. He calls this "misinvolvement," and describes an aspect of it as follows: "By looking at the ways in which an individual can be thrown out of step with the sociable moment, perhaps we can learn something about the way in which he can become alienated from things that take much more of his time."

The violation committed by many robopathic people in simple conversations may not be "misinvolvement" but "noninvolvement." Characteristically, robopaths interact by rote; they simply "press a button" and do their act in terms of their robot role. Their surface conversation is dedicated to image maintenance and may have very little to do with how the people really feel underneath.

In other terms, interaction between robopaths is almost pure ritual—without human content. In such social machines, interaction is ritualistic and mechanical. Behavior is normless in the sense that the rules no longer tend to have any real meaning for the participants in the interaction. They mechanically conform to norms that are not a true part of their human emotions.

Isolation

A fourth characteristic of alienation refers to isolation. A common case is the "intellectual" who becomes overly detached from the society and the culture. An increasing proportion of people in society are voluntarily and involuntarily isolated in this way. One significant literary portrait of this existential state of isolation and estrangement is found in Camus's classic novel *The Stranger*. The issues of alienation, self-estrangement, religious irrelevance, the family as a social machine, robopathology, and social death tend to converge in Camus's allegory of "modern man" as a robopathic isolated stranger.

The story line of *The Stranger* revolves heavily around a "blank moment" following a minor argument where the alienated hero kills a stranger on a lonely beach. In his subsequent trial, his condition of alienation is examined by the court as a vital force in what is viewed as a "senseless murder."

> Next, without any apparent logical connection, the magistrate sprang another question.
> "Why did you fire five consecutive shots?"
> I thought for a bit; then explained that they weren't quite consecutive. I fired one at first, and the other four after a short interval.
> "Why did you pause between the first and second shot?" . . .
> "But why, why did you go on firing at a prostrate man?"
> Again I found nothing to reply.
> The magistrate drew his hand across his forehead and repeated in a slightly different tone: "I ask you 'Why?' I insist on your telling me."
> I still kept silent.
> He told me he believed in God, and that even the worst of sinners could obtain forgiveness of Him. But first he must repent, and become like a little child, with a simple, trustful heart, open to conviction. He was leaning right across the table, brandishing his crucifix before my eyes.
> I started to tell him that he was wrong in insisting on this; the point was of quite minor importance. But, before I would get the words out, he had drawn himself up to his full height and was asking me very

earnestly if I believed in God. When I said, "No,"
he plumped down into his chair indignantly.

That was unthinkable, he said; all men believe in
God, even those who reject Him. Of this he was absolutely sure; if ever he came to doubt it, his life would
lose all meaning. "Do you wish," he asked indignantly, "my life to have no meaning?" Really I
couldn't see how my wishes came into it, and I told
him as much.

As the trial unfolds, it is revealed that the stranger's mother
had recently died and that he did not or could not cry at
her funeral. His machine-like relationship with his mother
becomes a focal point of his trial and this moral alienation
helps to convict him of murder. The judge proposed

to touch on certain matters which, in a superficial
view, might seem foreign to the case, but actually were
highly relevant. I guessed that he was going to talk
about Mother, and at the same moment realized how
odious I would find this. His first question was: Why
had I sent my mother to an institution?

I replied that the reason was simple; I hadn't
enough money to see that she was properly looked
after at home. Then he asked if the parting hadn't
caused me distress. I explained that neither Mother
nor I expected much of one another—or, for that
matter, of anybody else; so both of us became used to
the new conditions easily enough. . . .

Asked to explain what he meant by "my calm-
ness," the warden lowered his eyes and stared at his
shoes for a moment. Then he explained that I hadn't
wanted to see Mother's body, or shed a single tear,
and that I'd left immediately the funeral ended,
without lingering at her grave. Another thing had
surprised him. One of the undertaker's men told him
that I didn't know my mother's age. . . .

No sooner had he sat down than my lawyer, out of
all patience, raised his arms so high that his sleeves
fell back, showing the full length of his starched shirt
cuffs.

> "Is my client on trial for having buried his mother,
> or for killing a man?" he asked.
> And I tried to follow what came next, as the Prose-
> cutor was now considering what he called my "soul."
> He said he'd studied it closely—and had found a
> blank, "literally nothing, gentlemen of the jury."

The stranger was sentenced to death more for the crimes of
his isolation and alienation than for murder. Another theme
of the story was that he was to be guillotined not only because he had committed murder, but also because he confirmed the administrators of justice's suspicions of their own
ahuman qualities and the meaninglessness of their lives.
Thus, for these and other reasons, Camus's stranger—the
allegorical ultimate alienated man—was condemned to death.

Self-estrangement

A final element of alienation is self-estrangement. An extended psychological treatment of this version of alienation
is found in *The Sane Society*, where Erich Fromm writes:
"The person . . . experiences himself as an alien. He has
become, one might say, estranged from himself." The rates
of self-estrangement through drug abuse, psychosis, neurosis,
and crime reveal the escalation of self-alienation adjustments
in contemporary machine societies.

Alienation from the natural order is thus one characteristic
of a social machine. Another dimension is self-alienation or,
in other terms, identity problems. (This identity crisis phenomenon is more in the range of a neurotic adjustment, rather
than the previously discussed psychotic syndrome.)

People with identity problems very often escape from their
selves into a robopathic syndrome. When they are ritualistically conforming to the precise dictates of a situation—as,
for example, in the process of conforming in every detail to a
precisely defined and dogmatic religion—they often do not
have to confront their own self-estrangement.

Psychiatrist Karen Horney describes self-alienation as "the
remoteness of the neurotic from his own feelings, wishes,

beliefs, and energies. It is the loss of the feeling of being an active, determining force in his own life. It is the loss of feeling himself as an organic whole."

Fromm describes alienated man as one who "does not experience himself as the center of his world, as the creator of his own acts—but his acts and their consequences have become his masters, whom he obeys, or whom he may even worship."

The alienated person is out of touch with other people, his natural environment, and even spiritual involvement. Religious institutions have played a major role in this alienation and estrangement. Protestantism, in its attack against the power, dogma, and the ritual of the universal church, helped to free man for worldly activities; and, as Max Weber showed, provided moral support for rising capitalism. Great works resulted. But since Protestantism made man face God alone, without the community of the medieval church, and stressed the fundamental evil and powerlessness of man, a great price was paid for that freedom.

In *Escape from Freedom* Fromm observes that freedom usually carries with it an immediate sense of loneliness. Dependency on someone or something, even when it is a kind of bondage, *does* give one a sense of relationship. When people achieve a measure of freedom—as when leaving home for the first time, or obtaining a divorce—they automatically tend to experience a measure of isolation, loneliness, and even self-estrangement.

In a later book, *The Revolution of Hope*, Fromm posits the manner in which technocracies have helped to produce self-alienation, or in terms of this analysis, robopathology:

> In the search for scientific truth, man came across knowledge that he could use for the domination of nature. He had tremendous success. But in the one-sided emphasis on technique and material consumption, man lost touch with himself, with life. Having lost religious faith and the humanistic values bound up with it, he concentrated on technical and material

values and lost the capacity for deep emotional experiences, for the joy and sadness that accompany them. The machine he built became so powerful that it developed its own program, which now determines man's own thinking.

This issue of alienation in the mass social machine society was further expressed by philosopher Ortega y Gasset's statements that the masses have gained "complete social power" and that "the mass crushes beneath it everything that is different, everything that is excellent, individual, qualified and select."

In contemporary societies dominated by the political power of a mass robopathic "silent majority" who have elected their own robopathic leaders, this theme has special relevance. In this context people have become alienated from themselves, from nature, and even from the meaning of their labor. Alienation is thus a significant characteristic of contemporary societies and a pertinent concept in accounting for the escalating robopathic condition.

The unfortunate conclusion that must be drawn from this varied and random analysis of the observations of many significant thinkers on people versus social machines is that machines are winning the contest. At least at this time in human history, some of the most horrendous speculations and predictions about the negative impacts of technology on people are becoming social facts. People have become subservient to the social machines of their own creation.

4

IN SOCIAL
MACHINES

M odern mass society, the technocratic state, and their machine domination of people have grossly altered the patterns and styles of human interaction. Their ultimate impact has been the dehumanization of people to the point where much of their social interaction is machine-like. People's emotions, spontaneity, creativity, personal identity, and ability to be compassionate are increasingly reduced to a set of robopathic responses. This subtle social pathology infects all levels of human interaction, from interpersonal relationships in a primary group, such as family or love relationships, on through secondary groups, such as corporate and political associations. I am alleging, therefore, that technocracies and the machine way of life have transformed *human groups* partially and in some cases completely into *social machines*. A social machine is a dehumanized interaction system wherein people's relationships are relatively devoid of sincere emotions, creativity, and compassion.

SOCIAL MACHINE
CHARACTERISTICS

People* participating in humanistic groups are spontaneous and creative in their responses. They have a sense of self—of individual identity. Most important, they have a concern for and are compassionate toward other people. Participants in humanistic groups are capable of and can, in effect, love other people.

It is a central contention of this overall analysis that human groups in technocratic societies have, more or less, become transformed into social machines. Human interaction in social machines is dominated by a set of interrelated behavioral characteristics. In social machines, behavior is generally (1) robopathic, (2) status-dominated, and (3) egocentric.

Robopathic Behavior

This characteristic involves interaction that has limited spontaneity or creativity. The role-player is like a puppet who follows a particular set of prescribed and expected responses. Behavior is never new or fresh—it involves a frozen script. The actor's ability to be creative in relationships is reduced to

---

* Traditionally, the term *man* is used instead of *people*. Most social analysts tend to use terms like "mano Pate" or "man and his works," as if women did not exist. In accord with the meaning of this book and the recent and appropriate demands of women's rights groups, the term *people* has been used throughout. This is done because the total discussion is about people (male and female), and because the exclusivity of the term *man* tends to dehumanize women. This condition is part of the social machine malaise. It is interesting to note further that we are so accustomed to saying *man* when we mean men and women, that at points the word *people* seems to ring a discordant note.

zero in the extreme. After a time the role-player's creative ability becomes atrophied like any organ of the body that is no longer used.

In *social machine* interaction, people's needs and emotions become subservient to the ritualized frozen expectations of the social structure. People relate dominantly to each other's role or image. They suppress their real emotions and feelings to maintain their image. Trust of another person is virtually eliminated in the robopathic type of encounter that occurs in human groups that have become social machines. Inner thoughts and monologues are divergent from the overt conversation that is taking place. In a social machine, people are not truly interested in each other's personal welfare—although they mouth platitudes of concern.

In brief, therefore, in social machines interaction is robopathic in the sense that many of the words, gestures, and emotions expressed are dominated by the dictates and defined prescriptions of the machine system. The actor's personal feeling and motivations, spontaneity, or creative ideas are co-opted and virtually eliminated by the demands of interactions imposed by the social machine system.

Status-dominated

A group is a projected set of reciprocal statuses. The actor's status or position in a group defines responses to situations. In humanistic groups there is room for individual interpretations of a behavioral response. In social machines there is limited latitude for individuality. The extreme and common example of status- or position-dominated behavior is that of a worker's role on an assembly line. Workers adjust the rhythm of their bodies to the machines. For example, a particular worker's position stipulates that he turn a bolt twice as it comes past him on the assembly line. He is obviously status-dominated and must carry out this specific act or disrupt the whole assembly-line group system.

In a social machine all participants are reduced to the role of the caricatured "yes man." People are constantly aware of highly defined roles and respond according to the dictates of status.

They become interchangeable parts, cogs in a people assembly line, and they maintain a particular image. They must wear a mask that suppresses any individualistic emotions or personal identity behavioral responses. They may even dress alike, whether in overalls or in an expensive banker's gray suit. In this sense they are dominated by their status-position in the social machine and have lost their personal identities.

Egocentric

People in social machines are consumed with notions about correct or expected behavior. Consequently, they become self-involved or egocentric in the sense that they lose their compassion for other people in the human machine. Their empathic ability or humanistic urge to act on behalf of another person is reduced because other people in social machines are simply objects toward whom they act. Their only empathic motivation or need to understand other people's feelings derives from the selfish need to make a correct assessment of what their own behavior should be.

David Riesman's discussion of "other-direction" in *The Lonely Crowd* falls within this framework. The "other-directed" person is, in fact, egocentrically attempting to maintain an image. The child, according to Riesman, learns that "nothing in his character, no possession he owns, no inheritance of name or talent, no work he has done is valued for itself but only for its effect on others."

In the process of "other-direction" people do not really place value on other people's emotions or needs but only on the demands of their own status or image in the machine. They become the opposite of compassionate—they become egocentric. The central quality of egocentric behavior in social machines is therefore the loss of social conscience and concern. People function instrumentally rather than humanistically.

This quality is apparent in technological systems. It is perhaps most blatant in the interchange of technological machine products. As indicated, the sales process in a competitive system is relatively unrelated to social conscience. Most salesmen would, in fact, sell an Eskimo a refrigerator if it were at all possible. The T.V. sales-box creates all sorts of purchase motivations in people with practically no concern for their human needs as consumers. One of the blatant travesties is the sale of almost pure sugar to children in the form of a variety of no-food-value, colored, toy-packaged, sugar "crunchies."

Selling, a dominant theme in social machines, involves selling not only "things" but also one's self-image. The person becomes an image-item and each individual becomes consumed with being a valuable package. Being "in" in the sense of wearing the correct style and using "in" language nurtures self-involvement or egocentricism. This set of vain pursuits to conform to an image, look right, talk right, and be "in" further insulates individuals from being humanistically concerned with other people. (For example, most cocktail parties involve a conglomerate of people presenting their images in tired monologues that no one listens to.)

In social machines, therefore, people become dehumanized robots pantomiming ritualistic platitudes. Their identities become vague and amorphous in part because their external role-playing has lost contact with their interior emotions. The problem becomes one of maintaining a bright, effective, outer image at the expense of the individual's inner humanistic needs, motivations, and feelings.

The outer image often provides a convincing appearance of humanistic interaction. In the robopathic charade of a social machine, people may appear to be emotional, but the sound and fury of the social machine has limited human depth. In the extreme ideal-type plastic society all of the participants are robopaths whose lives have limited human value or meaning. In the *process* of enacting life roles the *form* of the acts takes precedent over the meaning of the enactments to the actor. The humanistic needs of the people acting on the life stage are submerged in the ritualistic forms that have become set patterns. Human needs become subservient to calcified or robopathic interaction forms. Some typical random enactments that have become standard roles in social machine societies may serve to illustrate the condition:

1. The robopathic politician who takes theatrical direction, gesticulates, fully controls and modulates his booming resonant voice, smiles, pounds the podium about surefire researched acceptable positions, and has no emotional involvement or value commitment to what he is saying.
2. The robopathic "lovers" who cry, plead, make gutteral noises, pledge total commitment, and are fundamentally uninvolved or committed to their immediate love object, since they generally trip from one flower to the next.
3. The social machine family that prays, plays, dines, talks, "loves," argues together—but whose members don't really communicate or have compassion for each other on any meaningful level of human interaction.
4. The social machine corporate organization that claims to be concerned about ecology, employee health and welfare, product excellence, "hiring its quota of minority people," and community service, but when confronted with a situation where financial profits compete with human interests, is automatically programmed to decide in favor of profit.
5. The robopathic salesman who dramatically claims to be selling a service or a fine product to satisfy the client's human needs, but who is basically programmed to sell his product for a profit, "by any means necessary." A reading of almost any textbook or article on salesmanship reveals a very limited discussion of ethics and recommends a commitment to the art of seduction. The consumer in the salesman-consumer social machine interaction is viewed as

a potential victim, rather than as a person. The salesman acting out a role that has zero compassion is not a sociopath, since he is legal, but he is enacting a robopathic role.

All of these standard role-players in social machines display robopathic behavior that is manipulative, status-dominated, egocentric, and acompassionate. These qualities of role-players in social machines pervade the interaction of both primary and secondary groups in a robopathic society.

PRIMARY GROUPS
AS SOCIAL MACHINES

In general terms a group is a system of interrelated statuses that operates in terms of certain defined norms for interaction. There are two general types: *primary* and *secondary* groups. *Primary groups* are more apt to be geared toward the gratification of the personal-emotional-humanistic needs of its members. *The family, for example, is considered a basic primary group.* The much-quoted statement of Charles Horton Cooley most succinctly defines a *primary group* as

> characterized by intimate face-to-face association and cooperation. They are primary in several senses, but chiefly in that they are fundamental in forming the social nature and ideals of the individual. The result of intimate association, psychologically, is a certain fusion of individualities in a common whole, so that one's very self, for many purposes at least, is the common life and purpose of the group. Perhaps the simplest way of describing this wholeness is by saying that it is a "we"; it involves the sort of sympathy and mutual identification for which "we" is a natural expression. One lives in the feeling of the whole and finds the chief aims of his will in that feeling.
> It is not to be supposed that the unity of the primary group is one of mere harmony and love. It is

always a differentiated and usually a competitive
unity, admitting of self-assertion and various appro-
priative passions; but these passions are socialized by
sympathy, and come, or tend to come, under the discipline of a common spirit.

A *secondary* or associational *group* is more anonymous and
is geared toward organizational or production goals. Secondary groups are not usually organized around people's
emotional-personal needs. A particular corporation, for example, is an association constructed for the end goal of manu-
facturing or selling a particular product. The occupant of a
role in a corporate entity is *expected* to be subservient to the
goals of the organization. Unlike a primary group, in a secondary group the person's humanistic needs are *expected* to
be secondary to the apparent goals of the corporate entity.

In this context, associational groups such as corporate organizations have no intrinsic commitment to serving the human
needs of the people who occupy roles on their system. To be
sure, there are well-planned, extravagant, public-relations
propaganda efforts directed toward proving that these organizations provide "good" working conditions and that the
corporate body "cares" about its employees—but it is apparent
that in these bureaucracies people are interchangeable parts in
the corporate social machine; and that the organization is
essentially geared to producing or selling a product and is not
dominated by the human concerns of its constituents.

In the corporate context, as indicated, the consumer of the
corporation's product is considered an inanimate object. The
consumer is the object of a market research that attempts to
determine his vulnerability to "colors" or to a particular advertising copy, rather than to determine his human needs.
This is true despite the feeble veneer of "institutional advertising" that tries to prove the corporation is constructed to
serve its customers' needs. It is generally apparent that the
corporate entity is a social machine in which *profit motives*
dominate any human motives. (Ralph Nader and his associ-
ates clearly reveal the ahuman, exploitative corporate motiva-

tions in such works as *Unsafe at Any Speed*, *The Chemical Feast*, and *The Vanishing Air*.)

Almost all secondary groups, therefore, such as corporations, military establishments, and governmental agencies, are social machines. Since the corporate entities in most technocratic societies are ahuman in their basic form, it is generally expected or at least hoped that people's emotional-humanistic needs will be gratified more fundamentally in primary humanistic group interaction. These would include such primary group constellations as families, lovers, communal and friendship relationships. In such humanistic primary groups at least three fundamental emotional-need traits are expected to be gratified:

1. *Self-identity.* In an ideal primary group, an individual feels a sense of selfhood. People are accepted because they "are"—they do not have to prove themselves in terms of performance. They feel part of an important human relationship. They can be completely honest and relax since they do not have to maintain an image that is not consonant with their inner self-identification. They are allowed to interact honestly and openly.

2. *Creativity:* People can be spontaneous in their interaction. They are free to act creatively with each other. There is no need to perform any of the precise functions that are dictated by the larger associations. People can test their inner feelings without the threats of repression or condemnation. This freedom fosters spontaneity, facilitates new, creative behavior patterns, and gives the person a sense of value and importance.

3. *Compassion:* People interacting in humanistic primary groups can express and receive compassionate responses. They can act toward each other in terms of the particular person rather than in terms of an egocentric or group-product goal. They can also receive the emotion of love for themselves as human entities. In a humanistic group people can interact for each other's emotional gratification

without conforming to any ritualized pattern or goal. They can interact in terms of the participants' humanistic needs and desires.

The degree to which these needs are *unfulfilled* is the degree to which a humanistic primary group becomes a social machine. In contrast with humanistic primary groups, *social machines* have limited freedom for people's sense of identity —people have highly defined status-positions in a social system. *Creativity*—their range of response is restricted to a particular circumscribed set of responses. And with regard to *compassion*—they are confined to *egocentric* and organizational motivations rather than to interest in other people.

An unfortunate conclusion that I would reach, therefore, from this overall analysis, is that secondary-association groups are, in fact, automatically *social machines,* and that increasingly many primary groups are currently veered in this ahuman direction. This is partially because most people's "human" interaction is dominated by spending considerable amounts of time in vast secondary group structures that are controlled by social machines.

SOME SOCIAL
MACHINE PATTERNS

Many groups give the overt appearance of being humanistic, vibrant, and spontaneous—when, in fact, they are dead social machines. A case in point is the overt appearance of many families. They often look and sound like happy, creative entities; then one day, to the surprise of many "close" friends, they break wide open with divorce, or in some rarer cases, with an unexplainable assault. The symptomatic explosion reveals and somewhat confirms the fact that the family was all along in reality a social machine whose visible part of the iceberg was loving and compassionate. Beneath the surface the participants were submerging and suppressing many feelings of frustration and hostility. The robopathic role-players involved were dutifully enacting their status-roles with overt compassion, but their true human feelings were suppressed.

There are a few dramatic cases of people living robopathic existences in social machines who one day break out into horrendous and extremist violent activity. These include boys who come from so-called good families and then one day erupt into atrocious homicidal assault.

A recent group phenomenon may also serve to illustrate acutely how surface appearance is often dissonant with the underlying meaning of robopathic behavior in a social machine. Recently, there has been a mass preoccupation with what might be termed *innovation groups*. These would include group therapy, sensitivity training, psychodrama, encounter groups, Synanon games, T-groups, nude therapy, and sensory awareness sessions. The dominant avowed theme of these approaches is that they are geared toward gut-level human interaction that activates humanistic feelings and lets "it" (these feelings) "all hang out." In most innovation group sessions people laugh, cry, "cop out" (express deep truths), and share their deepest emotions and feelings in an effort to break out of their restrictive robopathic shells. For the most part these methods are valuable and effective counterattacks for humanizing social machines.

There is, however, some evidence to support the position that the final irony of a social machine society may be that even these constructed "humanistic" social interaction patterns sometimes deteriorate into forms of interaction where some of the participants, who might be called "therapeutic groupies," cry, laugh, open up, and even have insights on cue. Some of these spontaneous "treatment groups" have paradoxically become therapeutic social machines.

Bureaucracy is a more obvious and openly admitted social machine that has reached epidemic proportions in contemporary society. Not only does it dehumanize the central cast of characters, the people who operate the machine, but it also has a major impact on people who must encounter its mechanical administration.

In the context of assaults on one's humanity, on the

simplest, most direct level, everyone has at some time become subjected to being treated as an ahuman robopath in a bureaucratic social machine. Several random examples may illustrate this condition.

The following is a real-life example of a war veteran's treatment in this context. After a series of phone calls, considerable appointment making, and maneuvering, he was in a face-to-face position with a Veteran's Administration bureaucrat who had the *subject's* files before him. The robopathic interaction in this bureaucratic social machine took this form:

> *Bureaucrat*:   Yes, according to our records, as a result of your service-connected tooth extraction we can replace your lower left molar; fill out these forms.

> *Client*: But sir, as you plainly see [he points to tooth] I have my lower left molar. It's my upper left molar that's missing and needs replacement. Take a look —here.

> *Bureaucrat*:   Yes, I see. That's very interesting. But according to our records and files, we can only replace your lower left molar and that's final.

It took a considerable amount of effort and letter writing to produce a situation where the client finally won over the bureaucratic social machine and had his missing tooth replaced.

Many of the functions of bureaucratic social machines are computerized. For the most part the machines work effectively. Yet when they run amok, as often happens, the client merely becomes a defective part in the machine system. The following exchange is an actual case example of a man versus a credit-card machine:

> *IBM bill*:   If you do not pay the past due bill attached, we will regretfully cancel your credit card.

> *Letter*:   Gentlemen: Enclosed is my check for the amount of the past due bill.

> *IBM bill*:   [Repeat of above plus a more severe threat.]

Letter: But I paid the bill last week.

IBM bill: [Repeat of above plus an even more severe threat.]

Letter: Please. Didn't you get my letter and my check two weeks ago?

IBM bill: [Repeat of above plus an even more severe threat.]

Letter: Please. Is there anyone human out there? Please respond.

IBM bill.:   [Repeat.]

Letter: Help!

A final irony may be noted in this example of children forced into social machine interaction in their most cherished fantasy:

SANTA IS ON THE TUBE

Instead of toddling up to a jovial, full-of-life Santa seated on a throne, children visiting the May Company Department Store here get their Santa on a television screen.

A store official said the live Santa Claus was "discontinued" to avoid the usual long lines of children waiting to see him.

The foregoing are minor examples of social machine tyranny. The issue is more complex in larger constellations such as cities and with seemingly useful machines such as automobiles. In these kinds of configurations, machines often assume greater importance than the people they are supposed to serve. Many theses about dehumanization identify certain obvious machines and the technocratic state as the arch-enemies of the people, as if these forces were produced on another planet and then imposed on humans. The obvious fact is that all of the social machine golems, dybbuks, and devils are produced by people. Ultimately, in this sense, the

technological products are part of the social machine interaction between people.
A symbolic and actual case in point is the subtle impact of
the automobile. The proud inventor of this initially fantastic
machine could never envision its ultimate effect. Because of it,
many large cities around the world have become slow guillo-
tine smog ovens. In recent emotional reactions, the automobile as a death machine is focused upon as the enemy. In a
burst of rage, a group of college students bought a new car,
hacked at it with pickaxes and then, symbolically, buried it in
the ground. This situation illustrates, of course, the ultimate
absurdity of displaced aggression. Obviously, people design,
manufacture, sell, buy, and drive these deadly machines that
are now very apparently beyond human control. The Franken-
stein machine produced and desired by people has simply
turned on its creators.

Even though the automobile, for example, appears to be a
technological atrocity, a machine monster imposed on people,
beneath the surface I am aware that I am fighting other
human beings over whom I no longer have any control. The
masters of the automobile and oil industries are slowly killing
people through their automobile weaponry. The vast industry
that assaults my lungs with carbon monoxide and other poi-
sons is ultimately in the control of people who administrate,
build, and sell the death-dealing devices.

They are as robopathically locked-in to their position of
killing as most people are alienated and robopathically powerless to stop them. This is a fundamental tragedy of the emergence of social machines. The robopathic inter-actors are often
invisible to each other.

The city is another example of people becoming hidden
enemies to each other in their social machine interactions.
The total complex and pattern of negative social machine
forces have become increasingly visible in the ahuman life in
the city. This social system that originally provided extravagant hope for the "good life" has had an enormous price tag
of dehumanization. The anonymity and abject loneliness of

the crowd in city life has been well documented. Other very manifest side effects of life in city social machines are crime, drug abuse (a necessary but devastating extremist adjustment), and retreat into the fantasy of psychosis.

The pollution of the air, water, and food by mass life in the city social machine has reached epidemic proportions. The crowding, the garbage, the smog, and the ersatz, refrigerated, processed, contaminated foods create a social poison that will, when escalated, provide the conditions for the mass extermination of large numbers of people.

Not all dehumanizing *social machines* necessarily have physical machine components. When people become secondary to technological needs, all sorts of dehumanization become valid. Racism is an example. Racism is a fixed social machine that enslaves both the "servant" and the "master." The social machine of racism locks the protagonists into a set of false premises that insidiously (slowly and totally) destroys many human lives. The *social machine* of racism dehumanizes the participants and places both the oppressed and the oppressors in absurd social positions that dictate equally absurd and ahuman patterns of interaction. Participation in the *social machine* of racism has produced such ignominious conditions as slavery, lynching, crime, varieties of violence, and a general dehumanization of the quality of life for vast numbers of people.

People vociferously deplore absurd social machine conditions, yet are apparently now powerless to modify certain emergent paradoxes. Consider the following seemingly immutable conditions that are railed against, but are quietly tolerated in almost all technocratic societies by people locked into robopathic roles that make them victims of their own social machines:

1. An economic social machine system where many people are overeating, storing food and fat, and other people are dying of starvation.
2. The escalation of size and complexity in educational social

machine institutions to the point where most of the participants in "the pursuit of knowledge" have limited the time and place for communication to abstract ahuman machine methods. (Large classes of IBM cards in cold, vast, sprawling concrete bunkers.)

3. The robopathic maintenance of social machines where one factor (e.g., skin pigmentation, caste, finances, sex, or ethnic origin) significantly determines people's positions, levels of aspiration, and the manner in which most people relate to each other. Thus, externally identifiable factors in the social machine determine the social interaction of people.

4. An internationally accepted commitment by major world political social machines to *escalate* the production of "fire power" for doomsday machines that can currently overkill (about ten times) hundreds of millions of people.

This latter point is one of the most potent examples of the social machine enslavement of people, since it has very apparent, potentially apocalyptic, consequences. These and other problems are increasingly *accepted* conditions of social machine-dominated societies. They emanate in part from a preoccupation with immediate sensate gratification from certain technological machines. The ultimate price paid is to place machine values over human existence.

The final absurd condition of human existence placed under the control of social machines that could potentially destroy all human life is found in the closer examination of smaller social systems. Part of the resultant epoch problem is that many people, out of fear and insecurity about their humanistic ability, begin to rely more and more heavily on planning, rituals, and the expectations of others in groups. In the process, their lives become cluttered with familiar repetitive patterns that very subtly obscure their vision and the reason for their being. As this escalates they become entrapped by expected *social machine* interaction patterns that dominate their lives. They give up their freedom of decision-making and creative choice to a routinized familiar pattern of relating, and in the process they reduce or even lose their ability to be creative in their interaction and group relationships. They radar-out the expectations of the situation and are thus robopathic in their behavior.

Even when robopathic behavior is a partial role, there is a carry-over from the social machine mode of interaction to primary group relationships. For example, the unscrupulous used-car salesman, or the "two-notch wrench turner" on the assembly line, or the "killer-trained" soldier cog in the army death-machine, cannot immediately shift roles and become a loving, compassionate husband or father when he leaves the social machine and relates to his family.

Primary group interaction has been the fountainhead for socializing and perpetuating the best humanistic tendencies of people. Its demise and conversion into a social machine in the technocratic state has virtually eliminated for many people the possibility of training, maintaining, and perpetuating their humanistic capacities. The technocratic state and the fear and loss of humanistic abilities have helped to produce a condition where increasingly larger segments of the population have become *robopathic, status-dominated,* and *egocentric role-players* in a vast array of *social machines.*

A CONCEPTUAL SUMMARY

A central theme of a social machine society is that it ultimately extinguishes the human spirit, and in this sense is suicidal and apocalyptic. The predictable consequence of all robopathic interaction in social machines is both the physical and spiritual annihilation of people. This could result in two possible ways: (1) Involvement with physical machines, without the controlled impact of humanistic values to guide technocratic growth, would ultimately destroy the natural ecological balance, or produce the uncontrolled doomsday machines and war that would physically kill people; (2) the uncontrolled, unaware development of ritualistically acting out roles in social machines would eventually produce a mass generation of robopathic people who would be the *walking dead*. Their existential quality of life would be reduced to basically irrelevant noises, the ingestion of food, and defecation. Any real appreciation of other people, art, and nature would be destroyed. The apocalypse would consist of millions of shadowy actors on a dead set.

There is no special preplanning that produces social machine societies. The resultant product is an unanticipated emergence that emanates in part from a lack of awareness. Humanistic groups tend *to drift* naturally toward calcification. It becomes easier for role-players to follow the paths of least resistance.

Spontaneity, creativity, and compassion in human interaction require involvement and thought. It is easier, in the short run, to follow the prescriptions for interaction precisely and without any interior questioning or gut-level, personal communication.

Another force that helps to produce and nurture social machine societies is a *fear* of the unknown or unexplained that seems to be a general human characteristic. A new or different human response requires a novel adjustment or reaction, and people generally seem to avoid change. Individuals in their natural growth or socialization process are constantly confronted with fearful new social situations, and it is always more convenient to take the path of action that is most familiar.

Fear also seems to be a force or reason for placing increasingly more confidence in machines. It is true that machines (physical and social) are generally more systematically reliable than people. The ultimate consequence of this reliance, however, is to erode the confidence and ability necessary for people to accept change and to be humanistically creative. The reliance on machine systems produces all sorts of machine-like intervening variables that separate people and reduce communication.

Social and physical machine tyranny begins truly to take over when people place a higher value on machines than on people and their humanistic value. In this context, cultural machines of the widest variety—e.g., automobiles, roads, oil, packages, houses, images, fashion, furniture, cosmetic body changes—tend to supersede and have a greater value than the people for whom they are intended. All of people's intrinsic needs for identity, a sense of creative ability, and the emotion of loving and being loved become secondary to the demands of the physical and social machines.

Machines are not the underlying problem. Social and physical machines are and can be valuable servants to a society's humanistic life style if they are contained and kept in a proper perspective. The question of human survival arises when the machines take over and begin, in subtle and blatant ways, to tyrannize people and their groups.

An *ideal type* or *total* plastic society would be one in which the participants would all become robopathic creatures totally controlled by social and physical machines. People's humanism, freedom of choice, and control over their life space would be zero. People would perform and conform in accordance with all the dictates of the machines. They would become, like the people in R.U.R., the prisoners and victims of their own robot-like creations.

In summary, in an *ideal type*, ultimate social machine society the following set of interrelated conditions, forces, and consequences would prevail:

1. People would be robopaths—devoid of identity, compassion, or any ability to be spontaneous and creative in their relationships or associations.
2. Humanistic primary groups would be transformed into social machines. The best qualities of people would be submerged in order to conform and perform to the highly defined rituals and prescriptions of social machines. Humanistic qualities like love and compassion would be submerged by feelings of hate and fear. Instead of people

interacting, in terms of their true emotions, robopaths would interact in relation to each other's status and image definitions.

3. The enormous complexity and number of alternatives and choices posed by social machines would ultimately produce frozen responses in people. Certain roles would become impossible to perform. People would be locked into bureaucratic boxes, powerless to perform any compassionate acts toward other people.

4. There would be a minimal possibility for human creativity. People would find themselves unfulfilled and frozen by a set of highly defined prescriptions for behavior. They would lose their ability to be spontaneous and creative. Existence would become robopathic, dull, and unproductive.

5. The physical machines created by people would tend to become authoritarian dictators of behavior rather than serve people as "memory banks" or vehicles for facilitating fundamental human motivations and development. Physical machines would dominate behavior, rather than people dominating the machines they had created.

6. People as robopaths would become alienated from themselves, other people, and their natural environment. The consequence would be an increased psychopathology and sociopathology that would only be eclipsed by robopathic behavior. Ecological destruction would escalate—since preoccupation with social machines produces a limited concern for the natural environment.

7. People as robopaths would have an overwhelming sense of anonymity, loneliness, alienation, and dissatisfaction with their society. They would be increasingly frustrated by the fact that they had no control over modifying or alleviating social problems that existed in their human orbit. The society would become increasingly segmented (not integrated) and move rapidly toward disintegration. Factions would ultimately fight each other violently from their circumscribed, polarized positions in the system.

8. A partial response to the robopaths' sense of powerlessness, acceptance of the escalation of the emergent violence. Violent crimes, war, poverty, and ecological destruction would be denounced overtly but accepted, if not facilitated, by unconscious suicidal motivations. People would become emotionally immune to the most horrendous disasters and destructive ahuman acts.

The central, potentially apocalyptic crisis of the twenty-first century may not be found in the highly publicized surface conflicts between East and West, "social" minority and majority groups, or left and right political factions. The crisis may fundamentally exist in the historical encounter in social systems between the counterpoints of *humanistic* and *social machine* forces. If people do not revive, maintain, and nurture their humanism, they may be doomed to an escalation (and covert acceptance) of physical death, or of the spiritual and creative death involved in a robopathic existence in a social machine society.

5

REACTION
FORMATIONS

We know by now that technology can be toxic as well as tonic. We know by now that if we make technology the predestined force in our lives, man will walk to the measure of its demands. We know how leveling that influence can be, how easy it is to computerize man and make him a servile thing in a vast industrial complex.

This means we must subject the machine—technology—to control and cease despoiling the earth and filling people with goodies merely to make money. The search of the young today is more specific than the ancient search for the Holy Grail. The search of the youth today is for ways and means to make the machine—and the vast bureaucracy of the corporation state and of government that runs that machine—the servant of man. That is the revolution that is coming.
—JUSTICE WILLIAM O. DOUGLAS

T he minority view of society as something ahuman, overly repressive, beyond bureaucracy, and the cause of alienation has been a historical preoccupation. The emergence of civilization, however, to the point where mismanagement may in time fully unleash the doomsday machines of totally destructive air and food pollution and overkill nuclear war, has never been a significant reality until the latter part of the twentieth century.

In order to overcome the varied, totally destructive crisis that now hangs like Damocles's sword over contemporary society, the decisions of people in power require—more than ever—relevance, flexibility, and wisdom. Yet it appears as if political leaders are increasingly robopathic and ahuman in their actions; and the major social institutions tend toward becoming increasingly inflexible social machines.

In this context, revolutionaries and dissenters are not *the problem*; they are merely actors or, at times, over-reactors to the situations they confront. The drop-outs and the disenfranchised revolutionaries may be viewed as a rebellious reaction formation to a pathology in the dominant social machine system. They are strangers in what is from their viewpoint an apocalyptic society.

The role of the stranger, as Alexis de Tocqueville demonstrated and as many sociologists—especially Georg Simmel—have pointed out, has always provided a valuable perspective on any society or civilization. Strangers have less of a commitment to the overall community. They are less guarded about revealing themselves and in turn people are more open with them. Mainly, however, because they are relatively less involved, they often see problems with pristine eyes.

In a brief but potent essay, Simmel pointed out that a person may be a member of a group in a *spatial* sense but still not be a member of the group in a *social* sense; that a person may be *in* the group but not *of* it. The "stranger," Simmel argues, is different from other group members in several sociologically significant respects. He is, among other things, more *objective* and more likely to be accepted as a *confidant*. He enjoys greater *freedom* from *convention* and is not restricted in his actions by "habit, piety and precedent."

There are increasingly many more "strangers" in social machine societies. They include *involuntary* minority groups whom the power structure has *placed* in a disaffiliated stranger position. Additionally, in the past decade, there have been increasing numbers of *voluntary* strangers—varyingly labeled drop-outs, dissidents, hippies, yippies, and revolutionaries. These young *voluntary* drop-outs—self-styled refugees from the affluent middle class who, under usual circumstances, would eventually occupy key leadership roles (doctors, lawyers, executives, politicians) in the inclusive society—have joined informally with black, red, brown, and poor *involuntary* drop-outs to become at times perceptive strangers of the dominant society.

Revolutionary and radical youth movements have become appendices to almost all contemporary social machine societies. These revolutionary movements have already in a subtle way significantly produced social change in such diverse areas as overall life styles (communes), political organization, fashion, police action, child-rearing patterns, judicial administration, and even legislative actions.

Perhaps the most significant impact of the revolution of dissent has been the excruciating soul-searching by the so-called "establishment" or people in power positions in the societies in which these movements have exploded. These group reaction formations have forced political leaders, people in industrial power, and even parents to examine the essential characteristics of the society they control.

Part of the self-examination is motivated by the fact that many sons and daughters of people in power have, in various ways, joined the revolution. They have had to reappraise critically the fundamental nature of "advanced," "civilized," technological societies. In this regard the revolutionary *reaction formation* of contemporary young dissenters has produced a valuable reappraisal of the fundamental structure of the society.

One widely read spokesman for the merits of this counter-culture is Charles Reich who, in his book *The Greening of America*, analyzes and cites some of the alternatives that are emerging and affecting the overall society. Central themes of Reich's analysis are that America has veered from its original humanistic purpose and that the "corporate state" has become a death-dealing machine. In examining America's earlier "levels of consciousness," he describes the manner in which America has moved off course. He first analyzes the drive that made it a corporate state and led it into becoming a death-dealing, machine-enslaved society. In Reich's terminology, *Consciousness I* involved the enormous promise of America and *Consciousness II* relates to the life style that emanated from the rise of the corporate state. *Consciousness III*, according to Reich, is the adaptation of the new young revolutionary and drop-out. It rests, he asserts, on various premises: respect for each individual, for his uniqueness and for his privacy; abstention from coercion or violence against any individual; abstention from killing or war; respect for the natural environment; respect for beauty in all its forms; honesty in all personal relations; equality of status between all individuals; genuine democracy in the making of decisions; freedom of expression and conscience.

"There is a revolution coming," he writes. "It will not be like revolutions of the past. It will originate with the individual and with culture, and it will change the political structure only as its final act." Reich asserts that "the revolution will not require violence to succeed and it cannot be successfully resisted by violence."

One characteristic of the revolution on the part of young, affluent voluntary drop-outs is a resistance to accepting the path of their parents in the plastic society. A conversation I had with a young hippie at the peak of the Haight-Ashbury life style provided some clues to this aspect of dropping-out:

> LY: Why are you here in all this violence and poverty? In a matter of 24 hours you could be in a big comfortable home . . .

Young man: I look up at my old man. He makes
$50,000 a year. My mom and dad have everything
you can want in this society. Yet I know they are both
miserable. They don't know how to talk to each other
or me. They probably ball once a month.
In other words, if I'm a good boy and do just what
my old man did—go to college, get good grades, run a
business, and become a success—I'll become as miserable as he is when I'm fifty. Later for that. It's bad out
here sometimes—but at least I'm trying something
different. I know where my old man's trip leads. I
don't know where I'm going now—but it's got to be
better. Dig?

The new youth movement of disaffiliation and rebellion
that originated in the 1960s and seems to be growing larger,
albeit different and more sophisticated in the 1970s, is both
a symptom of and a devastating commentary on the larger society in which it was spawned. Its origins and characteristics
mirror many of the frailties and defects of the more inclusive
system. When closely analyzed, the disaffiliation and disaffection of young people in such a system therefore provide a
valuable commentary on that very system. (Although the
analysis in this volume focuses on the United States as a case
example, there are apparent parallels in other technocratic
social systems in Europe, South America, Asia, and even
Africa.)
The emerging revolution encompasses all people who in
varying degrees have rebelled, disaffected, and sought life
styles alternative to the existing social structure. This would
include such diverse revolutionaries as hippies; yippies;
Weathermen (clear advocates of violence, including bomb-
ings); committed psychedelic drug trippers; black, brown, and
red power advocates; women's liberation organizations,
homosexual "gay" liberation; and, in brief, all segments of the
populace fundamentally opposed to the status quo in which
they feel (rightly or wrongly) deprived of their rights and
freedom. All of these individuals, groups, and organizations
are characterized by a disenchantment with the dehumani-

zation of the larger society and a subsequent involvement with alternative life styles which they believe are now or will become more humanistic.

Most of these movements are not spearheaded by any clear-cut, powerful leaders. They emerge more as a consequence of great unrest and frustration felt simultaneously by large numbers of people, predominantly young people. The movements emerged rather spontaneously. Many gathered momentum around slogans of LOVE and FREEDOM, and a rejection of middle-class materialism, hypocrisy, and dishonesty. The participants are running away from a society that offered them, from their viewpoint, limited hope for their humanistic aspirations.

The new coalitions' unifying awareness of the growing dehumanization produced by a machine society is aptly described by Justice William O. Douglas in *Points of Rebellion*: "The goal of their revolution is not to destroy the regime of technology. It is to make the existing system more human, to make the machine subservient to man, to allow for the flowering of a society where all the idiosyncracies of man can be honored and respected."

Part of the problem, he notes, is to be found in the "corporate state":

> First is the growing subservience of man to the machine. Man has come to realize that if he is to have material "success," he must honor the folklore of the corporation state, respect its desires, and walk to the measure of its thinking. The interests of the corporation state are to convert all the riches of the earth into dollars. Its techniques, fashioned mainly on Madison Avenue and followed in Washington, D. C., are to produce climates of conformity that make any competing idea practically un-American. The older generation has in the main become mindless when it comes to criticism of the system. For it, perpetuation of the corporation state and its glorification represent the true Americanism.

Many people who drop out seem to encounter the extreme conditions of the social machine's corporate state and its materialism. They appear to be overwhelmed and frightened by a social machine that spits out, in addition to products, enormous amounts of facts and figures. For affluent young drop-outs, the overwhelming number of alternatives and potential opportunities of the "robot" society turns them off. The possible choices of jobs, material goods, and other machine alternatives are increasing at such a remarkable rate that these youths feel a compulsion to turn off their relationship to the rapidly expanding and overwhelming machine. Their emotional and intellectual computers seem to freeze and lock when they play with the almost infinite number of choices offered them by the variety of social machines they encounter. In a reaction formation, many have tried to escape into mysticism, super-religiosity (often termed *Jesus freaks*), and drugs.

The dissent and reaction formation has taken a slightly different form for the poor and the racial minorities. The corporate machine has them blocked out of the middle and upper positions of the state. They are locked into the bottom strata of the machine system, and they can only acquire these lower level jobs if, and only if, they maintain a hat-in-hand posture toward the gatekeepers of the robot jobs on the assembly line. (In a recent article, "The Blueing of America," Peter and Brigitte Berger make the point that as upper-class youths drop out they leave more room at the top for lower socioeconomic positioned youths to move into upper positions in the social system. A provocative assertion.)

Minority people who have been involuntarily disenfranchised from the system in response to this condition have formed militant power groups of various persuasions. The Black Panther Party, for example, seems increasingly to attract young, black people to its fold. Part of the philosophy includes a militant, sometimes paranoid, form of self-defense. Their clenched-fist slogan of "by any means necessary" is an intrinsic part of a program designed to survive what they consider to be a genocidal intent of the majority.

The militant, sometimes violent nature of this group has influenced the methods of young white radicals. Unlike the more *retreatist* classic hippies, such diverse and transient groups as the yippies, white panthers, Weathermen, self-labeled "freaks," and other forms of young militants are more apt to aggressively *encounter* the system they find oppressive. The yippies, in particular, reflect and have articulated an unusual and unique pattern of revolution.

REVOLUTION AS THEATRE

The yippie battle pattern is encounter. Or, as one of their founding father role-models, Jerry Rubin, advocates: "DO IT!"

> We started yippie with an office, a mailing list, three telephone lines, five paid staff organizers, weekly general meetings and weekly Steering Committee meetings. We were the hardest workers and most disciplined people you ever met, even though we extol sloth and lack of discipline. We are a living contradiction, because we're yippies. Marijuana is compulsory at all yippie meetings.
> Yippies take acid at breakfast to bring us closer to reality. Holden Caulfield is a yippie. The Old Nixon was a yippie; the New Nixon is not. Yippies believe every nonyippie is a repressed yippie. We try to bring out the yippie in everybody. Yippies proclaim: Straights of the world, drop out! You have nothing to lose but your starched shirts! . . . Amerika says: DON'T! The yippies say: DO IT!

An important part of the yippie, then, is a psychodrama of the streets where encounter per se produces change. Rubin declares:

The goal is to turn on everybody who can be turned on and turn off everybody else. Theater has no rules, forms, structures, standards, traditions—it is pure, natural energy, impulse, anarchy. The job of the revolution is to smash stage sets, to start fires in movie theaters and then scream, "Fire!"

Abbie Hoffman, another founding father of the yippie reaction formation to social machines, echoes the same theme as Rubin in his book *Revolution for the Hell of It*:

Our message is always: Do what you want. Take chances. Extend your boundaries. Break the rules. Protest is anything you can get away with. Don't get paranoid. Don't be uptight. We are a gang of theatrical cheerleaders, yelling Go! Go! Go! We serve as symbols of liberation.

In the drama they stage, the "enemy" is involved—they make him a yippie. They enjoy right-wing political characteristics in their theater:

I dig fighting the right wing because they are up-front about what they do. They sensationalize, fantasize, and romanticize. To build *their myth* they exaggerate *our myth*—they create a Yippie Menace. The menace helps create the reality. They turn *us* into heroes. They set high standards for us to fulfill, and we become giants trying to fulfill their fantasies. The right wing are our theatrical directors.

In this context "the 1968 siege of Chicago" was in great measure produced by yippie Mayor Richard Daley and candidates and yippie collaborators Hubert Humphrey and Richard Nixon. The antagonists become the protagonists in the yippie street revolution.

The new youth revolutionaries, like most others, see themselves as part of the American system. Despite the conclusion of people on the right, yippie-type revolutionaries do not consider themselves part of a Communist plot. Rubin presents his Amerikan position as follows:

> I am a child of Amerika. If I'm ever sent to Death
> Row for my revolutionary "crimes," I'll order as my
> last meal: a hamburger, french fries, and a Coke. I dig
> big cities. I love to read the sports pages and gossip
> columns, listen to the radio and watch color TV. I dig
> department stores, huge supermarkets and airports. I
> feel secure (though not necessarily hungry) when I
> see Howard Johnson's on the expressway. I groove on
> Hollywood movies—even bad ones. I speak only one
> language—English. I love rock 'n roll.

Rubin describes an interchange with his Aunt Sadie that
delineates some of the differences between the old and the
new political left. He humorously collates the general perspective of many young revolutionaries:

> "Aunt Sadie, long hair is a commie plot! Long hair
> gets people uptight—more uptight than ideology,
> cause long hair is communication. We are a new minority group, a nationwide community of longhairs, a
> new identity, new loyalties. We longhairs recognize
> each other as brothers in the street.
> Young kids identify short hair with authority, discipline, unhappiness, boredom, rigidity, hatred of life—
> and long hair with letting go, letting your hair down,
> being free, being open." . . .
> "*Jerry, you have so much to offer*. If only you'd cut
> your hair. People laugh at you. They don't take you
> seriously."
> "Listen, Aunt Sadie, *long hair* is what makes them
> take us seriously! Wherever we go, our hair tells people
> where we stand on Vietnam, Wallace, campus disruption, dope. We're living TV commercials for the
> revolution. We're walking picket signs.
> "Every response to longhairs creates a moral crisis
> for straights. We force adults to bring all their repressions to the surface, to expose their real feelings."

"Feelings, schmeelings, Jerry," Aunt Sadie said. "I'm telling you that in my time we were radicals. We were invited to a convention in the Soviet Union to meet Stalin. And who did they pick to represent us? Who did they pick? I'm telling you who they picked. "They picked the people who were down-to-earth, who were clean and nice. I didn't have long hair. I didn't smell . . ."

"Aunt Sadie, I don't want to go to any fucking conventions," I said.

"That doesn't matter," she replied, suddenly pushing aside untasted her bowl of Nancy's good chicken soup. "But you should be clean and nice. Did your mother teach you to smell bad, maybe?"

"Aunt Sadie, you won't believe this, but you're uptight about your body. Man was born to let his hair grow long and to smell like a man. We are descended from the apes, and we're proud of our ancestry. We're natural men lost in this world of machines and computers."

Many of the seemingly diverse groups in the new revolution have a sense of camaraderie and brotherhood. They all adopted the long-standing black phraseology of "brothers and sisters" to denote co-revolutionaries. An important coalition in the revolution is the amalgamation of white and black. Eldridge Cleaver and many other black revolutionary leaders have come to view the white hippie-yippie factions as "brothers and sisters under the skin." Cleaver's comment that the new scene involves a condition where "the children of the oppressors have joined the oppressed" sums up this black militant view.

Jerry Rubin's view of Eldridge Cleaver's forced exile reveals the young white revolutionaries' concern and self-identification: "Amerika declared war on humanity when she exiled Eldridge. If Amerika is not free for Eldridge Cleaver, Amerika has no right to exist. The pigs fired the first shot. But we, the white and black niggers, will fire the last."

A central theme that seems to bind these and other diverse groups in the movement together is a sense of dehumanization, a sense of being a number, an IBM card, in a vast bureaucratic jungle of social machines controlled by a robopathic majority.

In this regard, black people in particular have more obviously been the direct victims of a prejudice that has given them an inferior, ahuman status in the society. In a more subtle way, however, many young, affluent whites have had a similar sense of the indignity of being dehumanized by educational and family social machines that indirectly and unconsciously rendered them helpless. They have limited confidence in the usual channels of communication; and many believe their call in the wilderness can only be heard if the volume is turned up and they use emotional rhetoric in a theater of the streets that has shock value.

VOLUNTARY AND INVOLUNTARY DROP-OUTS

Although a sense of dehumanization links these diverse groups, there are some significant structural differences between the revolutionary motivations of people who traditionally come from the lower socioeconomic positions in the society and people whose starting point is the upper stratum of the society. This issue can be best illustrated by examining the situation of what I will term *voluntary drop-outs* (e.g., hippies, yippies, et al.) in comparison with revolutionaries who start from an *involuntary drop-out* position (e.g., "juvenile delinquents," black and Chicano youths, and gangs).

The American ideology of "equal opportunity for all" is an empty phrase to those who find themselves blockaded from legitimate pathways to upward mobility and achievement in the society. Because lower-class groups are generally blocked from upward mobility, the pressures toward deviant behavior are greatest in this segment of society.

The traditional "delinquents"—lower-class youths who are almost automatically delinquent because of their cultural position and imposed life style—may therefore be accounted for in terms of the following set of conditions. The disparity between what lower-class youths are led to desire and what is actually available to them is the source of a major problem of adjustment. Faced with limitations on legitimate (legal) avenues of access to society's goals and unable to revise their aspirations downward, these people experience intense frustrations. This frustration often causes them to turn to a delinquent or deviant adjustment to try to acquire the goals (particularly materialistic goals) they have been led to believe are desirable. For example, if you can't get money because you can't get a job—you get the money with a gun; or you block out your desire for the money goal with dope.

Briefly, therefore, youths blocked from achieving through the normative avenues for success in an extremely achievement-orientated society often select a deviant path. The "deviant paths" for many lower-class youths are the traditional delinquent activities of violent gangs: drugs, assault, and theft. This traditional delinquent pattern has became an integral adjustment pattern for *involuntary drop-outs* in most modern technological societies. Blockages in opportunity channels for this segment of the populace have been a part of all societies of this type. There have always been have-nots who could not achieve the lofty goals aggrandized by their society.

In a sense, the goals and values of the society are confirmed by the fact that there are such people who will go to unusual means to win these rewards. Therefore, traditional delinquency (theft, robbery, etc.) in the modern technocracy is partial proof that the social structure's goals are still sufficiently attractive; and many young people in this situation will go to any means necessary—including theft and violence—to attempt to achieve the valued goals of the society.

Some traditional delinquents or *involuntary drop-outs* are so frustrated by not being able to achieve the success goals of the society that they retreat. In a sense, the old-style, drug-addict delinquents took drugs (and many still do) to console themselves about their lack of achievement of the valued goals of the society. "Traditional" ghetto drug addicts, in part, use drugs to escape from their failure to succeed in the plastic society.

This is in considerable contrast with psychedelic drug addicts who are trying to scramble their circuits to eliminate from their consciousness both the total social game-playing scene (the paths to achievement) and the goals of American society. They use drugs, in part, as a vehicle for dropping out of the social machines of the system.

In contrast with the sociodynamic situation of lower-class (involuntary drop-out) deviants, the new affluent deviants have excellent access to the goals of the society; they are not at all reacting to blocked opportunity structures. *In contrast with traditional delinquents, the new middle- and upper-class deviant revolutionaries reject the means, the goals, and the values of the society, and they are voluntary drop-outs.*

This devastating total negativity is partially reflected in a statement attributed to a Weatherman—the bomb-throwing arm of the revolution. The leader was asked what the Weathermen's program was.

"Kill all the rich people," he answered. "Break up their cars and apartments."

"But aren't your parents rich?" he was asked.

"Yeah," he said. "Bring the revolution home, kill your parents. . . ."

This middle- and upper-class deviant behavior and posture reflects a much more total attack on the basic structure of the society than the traditional delinquents' pattern. Traditional American delinquents *accept the goals* of the society even though they find it necessary to pursue them in a deviant way. *The lower-class American delinquent, therefore, is in a sense affirming the validity of the goals of American society by striving for them at any cost. Traditional crime and delinquency in this context are a tribute to the goals and values of*

American society. The new middle- and upper-class revolutionary reaction, in contrast, is a total condemnation of the social machine system.

Most youths who drop out into the new movement have access to and usually can have all of the cultural prizes of American society. Their condemnation and rejection, however, is total. They generally reject the basic institutions of family, religion, education, and government and the economic and materialistic prizes of the social machine society they are reacting against.

Their behavior in the courts provides a visible symptom of this increasingly total denunciation of the fundamental institutions by the dissenters. Defendants throughout history sat still during their trials, partly because they believed somewhat in the overall system—of which the judicial process was only an arm. If one believes the system is totally corrupt then, of course, the courts are also absurd. For example, Abbie Hoffman and Jerry Rubin put on judges' robes to mock the judge in their Chicago trial. For his irreverent response of complete defiance, Black Panther Bobby Seale had to be bound and gagged in the same Chicago "conspiracy" trials.

In another judicial event of total societal denunciation, a young black revolutionary, Jonathan Jackson, entered a courtroom with a sawed-off shotgun and tried unsuccessfully to release his "brothers." (Four people, including a "brother" and the judge, were killed in the subsequent melee.)

Rubin puts the new youth revolution's nihilistic and despondent philosophy in the following perspective:

> A good question: Can Amerika be changed through "peaceful transition"?
>
> Can the beast be tamed within her own rules and regulations? Within the electoral system, within law and order, within police permits and regulations, within the boundaries of middle-class Amerika?
>
> Can a society which makes distinctions between rich and poor, white and black, employers and employees, landlords and tenants, teachers and students,

reform itself? Is it interested in reform or just interested in eliminating nuisance? What's needed is a new generation of nuisances.

A new generation of people who are freaky, crazy, irrational, sexy, angry, irreligious, childish and mad.

people who burn draft cards and dollar bills
people who burn MA and doctoral degrees
people who say: "To hell with your goals"
people who lure the youth with music, pot and
LSD
people who proudly carry Viet Kong flags
people who redefine reality, who redefine the norm
people who wear funny costumes
people who see property as theft
people who say "fuck" on television
people who break with the status-role-title-consumer game
people who have nothing material to lose but their bodies.

All of these admonitions are recommendations for reaction-formations against a social system that is believed to be frozen and plastic.

THE ANNIHILATION
OF SOCIAL MACHINE INSTITUTIONS

Revolutionary people are urged to inflict outrageous, revolutionary, psychodramatic events against a social machine system they consider to be totalitarian and dead. The alleged plastic society they are attempting to pull down may be more closely appraised by examining its basic institutional patterns as social machines.

In the broadest sense of the term a social institution refers to an organized way of carrying out some fundamental function in a society. The basic institutionalized patterns of any society include (1) religious forms—ways of relating spiritually to other people, the universe, or God; (2) economic forms—the manner in which the wealth of a society is accumulated through work and then distributed; (3) the family—a human arrangement for experiencing a primary group, a loving situation that will properly procreate and socialize children into the norms and values of the system; (4) government—a patterned social organization granted the authority and power by individual citizens to administer many basic internal and external affairs or matters; and (5) education—organizations designed, through the pursuit of truth, to transmit fundamental knowledge in the arts and sciences from one generation to the next.

All societies have evolved institutionalized patterns for handling these basic human requirements. The existence and functioning of a social institution implies that individuals are willing to give up certain almost inalienable rights to a collective higher authority. In a real sense, to have a society with defined institutions requires that individuals be willing to give up a part of themselves.

A social contract is made with the elected leaders and their appointees by the society to administrate and manage certain dimensions of the citizens' life situation. The social contract implies that the authorities can control the freedoms of and punish those who violate the norms of the society, especially those norms written into law.

The new revolutionary movement involves a blanket total rejection of all of these fundamental institutions. Implicit in the new life style is not only a total rejection but also a statement that the laws promulgated by the society are ridiculous and no longer binding; and that the courts that administrate these laws are absurd.

The posture of *total rejection* places the new revolutionaries in a unique position. Historically, most small or even powerful social movements have been geared to modify only parts of the social structure. *The new revolution, although foetal and relatively powerless, emerges as the first social movement that totally rejects the social machine system.*

A *brief* appraisal of the counterculture's view of and revolutionary reaction to each of the basic institutions of American society tends to validate this observation.

Religion

For participants in reaction formations the spiritual and emotional quality of the religious experience in formal religions has died along with God. Churches and temples have become to the revolutionaries a materialistic mockery of an affluent society. Rather than catering to the spiritual and material needs of poor and disenfranchised people, most religious leaders (priests, rabbis, ministers) are viewed as quasi-businessmen, lawyers, accountants, and "social directors." (Many black revolutionaries view religion as a temporary opiate that blockades the mass of black people and prevents them from considering their enslaved and oppressed position.)

People go to church in expensive clothes and cars to show off their affluence. They are unaware and unconcerned with fundamental spiritual or religious emotions or experiences. Robopaths participate in a religious situation (when they do) as a matter of proper social machine form.

The white revolutionary youth movement tends to turn almost completely away from the "hypocritical Western religions" toward the Eastern religions. Despite their fragmentary knowledge, young people claim that the Eastern religions still emphasize LOVE, helping people, relating to God in one's own way, and most important, seeking a deep religious experience ("through drugs or meditation").

The only real Christian identification found by some is an involvement with the trials, search, and tribulations of Christ and the early Christians. Many fluently quote and read the New Testament. Also, the hip style of dress is often geared to the simpler clothes of the early Christians. In this regard some have become what has been termed *Jesus freaks*, spending their full time extolling and trying to live by the codes of the original Christian position. They do not consider themselves a part of modern Christianity.

Government

The dissenters generally view the rights and controls of traditional-formal government as absurd. The assumption that anyone should have real, granted power over another person is a complete violation of the new revolutionary ethic of "doing your own thing," being a "free man," and granting "Power to the People." (This accounts, in part, for the reaction formation against the judicial system and the "pigs" of law enforcement.)

A dimension of government that is considered "complete insanity" by the dissenters is the governmental power to make war and kill people. One of the most flagrant hypocrisies noted by the new leaders is the spectacle of an American government that talks peace and makes war. This governmental hypocrisy is deeply felt as an obvious indication of America's spiritual bankruptcy, and there have been many nonviolent and violent reaction-formations against war.

One bizarre and facetious view of government activity is expressed by Jerry Rubin in what he calls his Academy Award of Protest. It was written on the occasion of receiving a federal indictment for conspiracy:

> This is the greatest honor of my life. It is with sincere humility that I accept this federal indictment. It is the fulfillment of childhood dreams, climaxing years of hard work and fun. I wish to thank all those who made it possible. . . . I realize the competition was fierce, and I congratulate the thousands who came to Czechago. I hope that I am worthy of this great indictment, the *Academy Award of Protest*.

The Family

The American institution of the monogamous family is viewed by dissenters as an arid and sterile social machine. There is, according to them, no *real* love, no *real* communication, and no meaningful, satisfying sexual relations. Also, in the formal family they believe children are in bondage, without—as one stated—any real civil rights. Most base their viewpoint on their personal experiences in their own family.

Rubin lists the expectations of his family:

> Dad looked at his house and car and manicured lawn, and he was proud. All of his material possessions justified his life.
>
> He tried to teach his kids: he told us not to do anything that would lead us from the path of Success.
>
> | work | don't play |
> |------|-----------|
> | study | don't loaf |
> | obey | don't ask questions |
> | fit in | don't stand out |
> | be sober | don't take drugs |
> | make money | don't make waves |
>
> We were conditioned in self-denial.
>
> We were taught that fucking was bad because it was immoral. Also in those pre-pill days a knocked-up chick stood in the way of Respectability and Success.
>
> We were warned that masturbation caused insanity and pimples.
>
> And we were confused. We didn't dig why we needed to work toward owning bigger houses? bigger cars? bigger manicured lawns?

In the context of the traditional American family's values, the new freedom in sexual expression is considered promiscuous and pornographic. The promiscuity, bordering on orgy, is a partial expression of the revolution's reaction-formation against "the family" as a social machine.

The sexual freedom of the movement is in part an extremist reaction formation to the covert and guilty sexual practices of the average middle-class family. Sex in the new revolution's "families" and communes is definitely freer and more wide open. Couples often have sexual intercourse in view of other members of their "tribe." This dramatic reaction to middle-class mores may be another way they blatantly declare their "freedom" from the middle-class bankrupt institution of the traditional family they personally experienced.

Economic

The plastic society's competitive system of free enterprise and capitalism is clearly rejected by the new movement. For example, affluence is consciously and often methodically replaced by poverty in the movement. As one young girl in the East Village commented: "I dropped out because I wanted to experience the emotion of poverty." She came from an extremely wealthy family in the Midwest. (Revolutionary Weatherwoman Diana Oughton's life style of abject poverty was a clear attack on her family's affluence and wealth.)

The most definite statement by the new deviants that is related to America's vast and powerful economic institutions is their life-style declaration of rejecting social machines and game-playing. They are attempting to move from America's great industrial, technological, and economic system back to the land and to an agrarian way of life. This is clearly evidenced in one pattern of a valiant but generally unsuccessful attempt at farming, making one's own clothes and food, and the natural life efforts in rural hip communes.

Education

The revolutionaries' view of the hypocrisy of the American educational megalopolis is most clearly evidenced by the escalating college drop-out pattern, by white radical and black student group revolt, and by the ferment that often turns to violence on campuses. A majority of the new affluent white deviants have experienced the college or university life and then dropped out. Some dramatically demonstrate their strong negative reactions by going through a university up to their senior year and then quitting the system.

The major complaint is that they feel they are IBM cards

in a social machine educational system. They do not want "to be folded, spindled, or mutilated by the machine." Large, anonymous, irrelevant classes; professors disinterested in teaching or relating personally to students; and ahuman, compulsive, robopathic administrators give them their rationale for leaving the cold bureaucratic educational system, or using the university as a revolutionary staging area. In extreme cases of reaction, buildings have been destroyed by bombs.

Another view expressed by many youths about higher education is that it educates people only to perpetuate the social machine society of which it is an integral part. The emphasis is on acquiring knowledge to "fit in better" and to learn robopathic conformity to the system's social machines. The quest for truth, the "holy grail," or for knowledge-for-the-sake-of-knowledge, is dead in American education, according to the revolutionary drop-outs.

Jerry Rubin describes the overall rejection scene of America's alleged social machine institutions in this way:

> What's happening is energy exploding in thousands of directions and people declaring themselves free.
>
> Free from property hang-ups, free from success fixations, free from positions, titles, names, hierarchies, responsibilities, schedules, rules, routines, regular habits.
>
> I'm not interested in the so-called antiwar movement—I'm interested in Detroit, Newark, campus disruptions, everyone smoking pot, people learning to speak out and be different.
>
> The capitalist—money—bureaucratic—imperialist —middle-class—boring—exploitative—military— world-structure is crumbling. . . .
>
> All these movements for liberation add up to a massive energy force which weakens the ability of the U.S. to carry out the war and all her other decrepit policies.
>
> I support everything which puts people into motion, which creates a disruption and controversy, which creates chaos and rebirth. . . .

> The stable middle-class home is falling apart.
> The church cannot attract its own children.
> The schools are becoming centers of rebellion, and
> the streets are theaters of political action. . . .
> That is guerrilla war in Amerika: everyone doing his
> own thing, a symphony of varied styles, rebellion for
> every member of the family, each to his own aliena-
> tion.

The revolutionary movement fundamentally comprises an encounter with and an attack upon a social machine system that inhibits spontaneity, creativity, and lacks compassion; a society that is alleged to be dysfunctional for people. It is an outrageous and bizarre set of reaction formations that includes not only socially and economically disenfranchised participants but also many people who are the heirs apparent to the power, wealth, and status they are trying to destroy.

One apparent paradox of the revolution against the social machine society is that in the process some revolutionaries seem to lose their humanistic compassion and to create their own destructive organizational social machines. Many revolutionaries and dissenters have acquired the same ahuman qualities of the robopathic leaders of the society they are attempting to destroy.

6

THEMES
OF DISSENT

The rebellion of both *voluntary* and *involuntary* drop-outs is largely against social machines. A considerable part of the revolutionary movement emanates, however, from other motivations. Many rebels attach themselves to the movement because of personal frustrations and problems that have little or no ideological foundation. Historically, extremist social movements have always become rallying points for people uncommitted to the inclusive society. They have been motivated by a variety of reasons other than a sincere disaffection with the system.

Eric Hoffer, in his excellent analysis *The True Believer*, identifies—among others—two pertinent characteristics of joiners of social movements. He contends that they are generally dissatisfied, alienated, and frustrated participants in the formal society who are looking for a change: "It is a TRUISM that many who join a rising revolutionary movement are attracted by the prospect of a sudden and spectacular change in their condition of life."

People who join social movements tend to manifest characteristics of discontent, frustration, and alienation. They believe, perhaps correctly, that the institutionalized social system holds no promise of fulfillment for them. They are, in essence, "turned off" by the more inclusive society. In this regard, according to Hoffer,

> a rising mass movement attracts and holds a following not by its doctrine and promises but by the refuge it offers from the anxieties, barrenness and meaninglessness of an individual existence. It cures the poignantly frustrated not by conferring on them an absolute truth or by remedying the difficulties and abuses which made their lives miserable, but by freeing them from their ineffectual selves—and it does this by enfolding and absorbing them into a closely knit and exultant corporate whole.

Another general characteristic of mass movements that is relevant to some participants in the new revolutionary scene is an *extravagant faith* in the new order and an assuredness of victory against great odds. Participants often have an unshakable belief in the correctness and perfect character of their new life style. In brief, fanaticism is another general characteristic of reaction-formation revolutionary movements. The self-appointed high priests of the new movements are often megalomaniacal in their belief. Abbie Hoffman comments:

> Revolution for the hell of it? Why not? It's all a bunch of phony words anyway. Once one has experienced LSD, existential revolution, fought the intellectual game-playing of the individual in society, of one's identity, one realizes that action is the only reality; not only reality but morality as well. One learns reality is a subjective experience. It exists in my head. I am the Revolution.

For some youths on the new scene their *extravagant faith* often compensates for an underlying sense of insecurity and emptiness. Such alienated people in the mass social machine attempt to throw themselves into the arms of omnipotent new movements. Hoffer's observations on the fanaticism of *The True Believer* is revealing: "The fanatic is perpetually incomplete and insecure. He cannot generate self-assurance out of his individual resources—out of his rejected self—but finds it only by clinging passionately to whatever support he happens to embrace." This passionate attachment is the essence of a blind devotion and religiosity that becomes a source of "virtue and strength." Though the single-minded dedication may be a holding on to some semblance of their lives, they tend to see themselves as supporters and defenders of a holy cause.

This dedication or fanaticism often accounts for the kamikaze quality of some revolutionaries. (For example, in a march against the war, a young man committed to revolution told me that he was prepared "to kill or be killed by the pigs.") This expectation of possible self-annihilation is an important part of the revolutionary fervor, as well as being a suicidal characteristic.

A large proportion of participants in the revolution have arrived at their philosophical position and a subsequent line of action on the basis of cold analysis, intellectual discussion, and introspection. Many intellectually and emotionally perceptive people, young and old, confront what they see as a social machine society and then, on the basis of their personal reasoning and rationality, decide systematically to produce social change.

Such movements, however, are also attractive to many young people who have become emotionally disturbed by attempting to live in the social machines of the society. They gravitate to a radical drop-out life style because it offers a potential vehicle for solving their emotional problems. For them and others it is a more convenient adjustment than accepting the "neurotic" or, in some cases, "psychotic" label and treatment they would receive from the formal society. On the new scene, their pathology or social inability is responded to with greater tolerance and in many instances with greater understanding and helpful attention from their peers.

"The revolution" in these cases is simply a *shield of immunity* that allows some people to act out violent and bizarre behavior emanating from psychodynamic sources; and this cloaked behavior has little to do with effecting social change. The revolution merely provides a more "rational" and justifiable *shield of immunity* for expressing emotions that have a psychogenic base that is possibly related to a social machine family.

Many revolutionaries therefore, due to emotional problems, fail as participants in the larger society. The revolution provides a syndrome and a haven that affords them some respite from their personal problems and the immediate pressures of membership requirements in oppressive social machines.

EMOTIONAL DROP-OUTS

The drift, therefore, by some people into the new scene is not always exclusively motivated by noble reaction formations against the social machines of the society. Some rebels are emotionally disordered in the usual meaning of the concept.

According to Norman Cameron, who has written about the general problem of psychological drop-outs, "they become socially disarticulated and very often have to be set aside from the rest of their community to live under artifically simplified conditions." The revolutionary role may serve as a "simplified" withdrawal syndrome for "disarticulated people" who drop out from the inclusive society.

With a concept called the "paranoid pseudo-community," Cameron attempts to account for this complex drop-out pattern:

> As he begins attributing to others the attitudes which he has toward himself, he unintentionally organizes these others into a functional community, a

group unified in their supposed reactions, attitudes, and plans with respect to him. He in this way organizes individuals, some of whom are actual persons and some only inferred or imagined, into a whole which satisfies for the time being his immediate need for explanation but which brings no reassurance with it and usually serves to increase his tensions. The community he forms not only fails to correspond to any organization shared by others but actually contradicts the consensus. More than this, the actions and attitudes ascribed by him to its personnel are not actually performed or maintained by them; they are united in no common undertaking against him. What he takes to be a functional community is only a paranoid pseudo-community created by his own unskilled attempts at interpretation, anticipation, and validation of social behavior.

Cameron's description fits people who, due to a set of complex forces, have become emotionally disarticulated. Although many revolutionaries manifest this syndrome, many others are sincerely involved in a reaction formation against a social machine society. They are people turned off from relating to an establishment that has given them a sense of being dehumanized and ahuman. They feel an overpowering need to break out of their cast robopathic roles. They could, but do not, have the desire to succeed according to the machine's conditions of success. They thus reject and drop out of the formal society and join a movement that seems pitted against the enemy. They have the extravagant faith that the revolution will produce the social change necessary and that their life condition, and others', will be radically modified in a humanistic direction.

NEAR-GROUP PHENOMENON

A characteristic of many nonconformist organizational forms is that they are not coherent, identifiable groups; nor are they simply random crowds or collectivities. They are what elsewhere I have termed *near groups*.

Unlike true groups, near groups characteristically have the following properties: (1) The roles of members are not precisely defined; (2) the collectivity has limited cohesion and tends to be impermanent; (3) there is a minimum consensus among participants about the entity's norms; (4) the members and participants are constantly shifting; (5) leadership is emotional, transitory, and often vague. *All of these factors seem applicable to the various organized factions of dissent.*

Another dimension of the near-group concept applicable to the new scene is the fact that there are differential levels of commitment to the movement. There are both *core* and *marginal* participants. In the revolution there are both "sometime" participants, and total drop-outs. Most formal groups have a greater consistency of commitment. Members are clearly committed and belong to the group in more uniform ways. In near groups there is a greater allowable range of involvement or commitment.

The near-group nature of the revolution is apparent. At revolutionary conventions or counterculture events there is often a high level of confusion about membership definition, leaders, the norms of the collectivities, and, at times, even about goals. This disarticulation is also evident in the exaggerated, changing, and distorted characteristics of the organization presented in the newspaper arm of the revolution, its underground press. Many emotionally stable and ideologically sincere revolutionaries deplore the chaos of most organization meetings and some drop out of the rebellion for this reason.

The near-group revolutionary movement of both reality and unreality has become for many participants a convenient pseudo-community: a functional community that at least temporarily alleviates feelings of personal inadequacy, encourages the ability to perform creatively, and offsets the need to participate in the oppressive straight society. The structure of the near-group situation of revolution and happenings, with its flexibility of size, roles, and some delusionary possibilities, makes it a most convenient and socially acceptable escape route from a vast empire of oppressive social machines.

Drugs as a
REACTION FORMATION

Drugs are widely and regularly used on the drop-out scene. In fact, an important starting point for contemporary movements and perceptions of the oppressive nature of social machines may very well have come from the ingestion of psychedelic drugs in the early 1960s. Despite the variety of negative consequences of drug use, it has apparently enlarged and changed the vision many young people have of their existential state and the ahuman social problems of this century. The advent of psychedelic substances and their increasing use by many segments of the population has produced far-reaching impacts on the perceptions and life styles of millions of people.

The random use of psychedelic substances began prior to 1960; however, it was around that time that Drs. Timothy Leary and Richard Alpert began their "Harvard drug experiments." Leary's (now platitudinous) admonition to "turn on, tune in, and drop out" progressively captured the imaginations of several million young people during the 1960s.

Many began to experiment daily with mind-altering substances such as LSD, peyote, and especially marijuana. A significant consequence of these earlier experiments was the evolution and development of alternative life styles and a different perception of the world. Hippie communal colonies began to emerge in both urban and rural areas. The use of psychedelic drugs has become an established part of the new youth society.

Mind-altering drugs, especially LSD and marijuana, have become vehicles that are used consciously for dropping out of what was then and is now varyingly referred to as the "plastic," "dehumanized," or "machine" society. The drug users' perspective on the aggrandized technological society differs from that of the general population. "Heads" (chronic psychedelic drug users) do not view society in the same way as most citizens. More specifically, the "heads'" view of society has become progressively almost entirely different from people in the power structure. "Heads" have turned on millions of non-heads to their view of the world. Many believed, at least for a time, that they had achieved a new relationship to themselves, other people, and nature. Some felt that they had achieved a transcendental state of cosmic consciousness.

As partial consequence of turning on to drugs and dropping out, the "new strangers" have developed, as described, a variety of different observations. Among other issues, for them: formal education is irrelevant; man is destroying himself through pollution of the environment; technological products are distributed in an absurdly inequitable way; war is atavistic and useless; and most political leaders are ahuman robopaths. As one hip philosopher stated to me:

> This culture with all its values, mechanisms, and industrialism is just something that came along in the last hundred years, and it is essentially unsatisfying even to those who are extremely successful. There are millions of people who are not now and never were caught up in this particular plastic society. What is going to endure is the Universal society of nature that underlies all of this crap we see on the surface. This is one of the important realizations you have under drugs.

COLLECTIVE BEHAVIOR PATTERNS

Psychedelic drugs served as a vehicle for attempts to drop out of the social machines of the plastic society. Another vehicle that produced insights and a coalition of people for rebellion were the mass group happenings that occurred heavily in the 1960s and persist in the 1970s. At these events people meet and share ideas with people of like minds. The massive event tends to validate and confirm the individual's perceptions of the other social machine society and provides people with a sense of identity and belonging to a relevant group. They feel part of a viable entity that may help produce the social change they desire.

In this context, Kurt and Gladys Lang—in a discussion of "crowds"—make a relevant point when they comment that certain aspects of a group situation help to make deviant acts and emotions more generally acceptable:

> The principle that expressions of impulses and sentiments are validated by social support they attract extends to collective expressions generally. The mere fact that an idea is held by a multitude of people tends to give it credence.
>
> The feeling of being anonymous sets further limits to the sentiment of responsibility. The individual in the crowd or mass is often unrecognized; hence, there is a partial loss of critical self-control and the inhibitions it places on precipitate action. There is less incentive to adhere to normative standards when it appears to the individual that his behavior is not likely to provoke sanctions against him personally . . . each person sees himself acting as part of a larger collectivity which by inference, shares his motives and sentiments and thereby sanctions the collective action. In this sense the crowd is an excuse for people all going crazy together.

The scenes of dissent include large-scale be-ins, marches, rallies, riots, music festivals—situations where size and power are dramatically present. Rubin views such gatherings as situations where young people can simply "be," in an existential sense:

> All of that energy in one place at one time was the Atom Bomb explosion of the youth culture. The Be-

in: a new medium of human relations. A magnet
drawing together all the freaky, hip, unhappy, young,
happy, curious, criminal, gentle, alienated, weird,
frustrated, far-out, artistic, lonely, lovely people to the
same place at the same time. We could now see one
another, touch one another and realize that *we* were
not *alone*. All of our rebellion was reaffirmed.

The most dramatic example of the large collective scene
was at Woodstock, New York. Large-scale rock festivals like
Woodstock reveal some of the dynamics of this dimension of
the revolution.

The assumption that music is the dominant theme of such
gatherings is a false one. Music is the backdrop. It serves, as
in all cultures, to validate, reinforce, and illuminate the
counterculture. One real purpose of the festival is a gathering
of the tribe, a getting together of people of like mind. Essentially, it bears some resemblance to a formal meeting of a
professional association. People at the festivals do not hold
seminars on how to smoke or use dope, resist arrest, make
bombs, handle an abortion, or how to deal with the "pigs";
but they do communicate informally about these subjects and
generally about how to live another (albeit revolutionary)
life style within the framework of the social machine society.

Tribal gatherings also validate the size of the movement by
making it visible. Collective events help to crystallize a lot of
inarticulate feelings, moods, and structures; such events validate for participants their massiveness and power. It seems
important for people who feel alone, smashed down, *possibly*
on the wrong track, to find others who share their position
and their attitudes toward dope, sex, and the obscene machine
society.

At these collective events the norms of the rebels prevail.
Each gathering becomes an opportunity for a mass of people
to test out the new life style. The plastic society's written and
unwritten laws are suspended for the duration. At Woodstock-
type festivals, for example, drugs are hawked like hotdogs at a
football game. Anything goes in dress, nudity, sexual behavior,

and language. If police had enforced the laws on "indecent exposure" or drugs at Woodstock, for example, they might have filled every jail in the state of New York. The revolutionary communities' norms and laws prevail on the collective mass scene. It becomes normative and "legal" to smoke pot, be nude, and "do one's thing." The police are handcuffed and the external society is disabled at least temporarily by the mass nature of the movement. The results of the revolution and its vaguely proposed alternate life style are thus confirmed by the mass collective enterprise.

COMMUNAL IDENTITY

Many new leaders believe, as one stated, that "basically we want to return to a closer relationship to nature and escape the plastic society." This goal, as many ecologists proclaim, seems crucial in a technological society that has choked the land with city and highway overuse, and with the same energy has filled the air with deadly smog. The communal life style is an attempt at relating to the environment in a more natural way, finding one's self-identity, trying to live creatively and compassionately in a small, humanistic group.

The concept of a small commune rejects the vast, anonymous (secondary group) mass of faces in the crowd found in American society. The dream of communal revolutionaries is to return to the tribal position of the Indian or to the more satisfying life of a more closely-knit extended family: a situation where adults and children can live more intimately and humanely in a cohesive, face-to-face primary group. One long-term communal member described it this way:

> I think the people are missing the point, because they confuse money with real wealth. They spend a lifetime working for a future that never comes. Here you do have an opportunity to create your own style. How do you define real wealth? Real wealth is something we have in abundance. We eat better, we

breathe better air, we live in more beautiful surround-
ings, with people we like and respect. That's real
wealth to me.

Another idealized characteristic of the communal way of
life is a self-contained, subculture economy. Jerry Rubin comments:

Our youth ghettos must have a communal economy
so we can live with one another, trading and bartering
what we need. A free community without money.

We will organize our own record companies, publishing houses and tourist companies so profit will
come back into the community for free food, free rent,
free medical care, free space, free dope, free living,
community bail funds.

Thousands of us have moved from the cities into
the country to create communes. Dig it! The communes will bring food into the city in exchange for
services which the urban communes will bring to the
country.

We will declare war against landlords and liberate
homes and apartment buildings for people who live
in them.

We will police ourselves.

And arm ourselves against the pigs who come into
our communities to wipe us out.

We are creating our own institutions which will
gradually replace the dying institutions of Amerika.

The communal, separatist view is not held exclusively by
hippie-yippie white youths. Blacks and other revolutionary
groups have also discussed and debated the merits and de-
merits of separatism.

SOCIALIZATION
OF CHILDREN

Every human system has to evolve a method for socializing
its young. The counterculture philosophies dictate alternate

patterns of child-rearing; these are being crystallized in a reaction against the dominate social machine approach that produces robopaths. The following statement about bringing up children in a commune made by an advocate of the new scene depicts the counterculture view of socialization:

> I maintain that children are born with a spiritual consciousness. The effect of this culture's ignorance of the nature of a spiritual life is to render us incapable of knowing or accepting spirituality in infants and children. The culture and homes into which children are born are devoid of a spiritual atmosphere. Competition, status and materialism are watchwords. Children are given plastic toys, and the television set is the national babysitter. A spiritual atmosphere is characterized by a deep respect for all forms of life, a recognition that all is perfect because it IS the present manifestation of Life, not in potential, in the fantasy future, but NOW. Infants and children are not respected. They are treated as slightly imbecilic and moronic, a different species to be guided along until they become like adults.

He goes on to point out that "adults should not lay their trip on kids," especially not in the "circumcision violation, or in any other areas." In brief, he almost calls for a total parental hands-off policy and for treating the child as an adult's equal in interaction. His viewpoint is representative of many contemporary hip parents who are reacting against social machines, trying to see to it that their children do not emerge as robopathic game-players.

Jerry Rubin advocates the necessity of both freeing young people from the old system and having them join the new:

> Everything the yippies do is aimed at three-to-seven-year olds.
> We're child molesters.
> Our message: Don't grow up. Growing up means *giving up your dreams.*
> Our parents are waging a genocidal war against

their own kids. The economy has no use or need for youth. Everything is already built. *Our existence is a crime.* . . .

The function of school is to keep white middle-class youth off the streets. *High schools and colleges are fancy babysitting agencies.*

Vietnam and the school system are the two main fronts in Amerika's genocidal campaign against the youth.

Jails and mental hospitals follow closely. . . .

Republican fat-cat businessmen see their kids become S. D. S. leaders. War profiteers' children become hippies. Senators' kids are arrested at pot parties.

Generational war cuts across class and race lines and brings the revolution into every living room.

The revolution toppled the high schools in 1968. Soon it will go to the junior highs and then the grade schools.

The leaders of the revolution are seven-year-olds.

WORK AND MONEY

The dissenters' posture parallels Thoreau's view of work:

Most men, even in this comparatively free country, through mere ignorance and mistake, are so occupied with the factitious cares and superfluously coarse labors of life that its finer fruits cannot be plucked by them. Their fingers, from excessive toil, are too clumsy and tremble too much for that. Actually, the laboring man has not leisure for a true integrity day by day; he cannot afford to sustain the manliest relations to men; his labor would be depreciated in the market. He has not time to be anything but a machine.

This view of work in a megamachine society, cogently described by Thoreau, parallels the new viewpoint. They abhor the "Protestant ethic" generally adopted by American middle-class society. The "Protestant ethic," as presented by sociologist Max Weber, makes a religious virtue of individualism, frugal living, thrift, and the glorification of work practices that favor the accumulation of wealth.

The dissenters generally consider "nine-to-five work" in the technological social machines of the society as spiritually harmful. They find it brutally dehumanizing. They believe, as Paul Goodman states in *Growing Up Absurd*, that most occupations and work in contemporary machine societies are irrelevant and absurd. Goodman writes:

> Economically and vocationally, a very large proportion of the young people are in a more drastic plight than anything so far mentioned. In our society as it is, there are not enough worthy jobs. But if our society, being as it is, were run more efficiently and soberly, for a majority there would soon not be any jobs at all. There is at present nearly full employment and there may be for some years, yet a vast number of young people are rationally unemployable, useless.

Counterculture people may be Veblen's avant-garde leisure class in an automated society. One hippie leader, for example, commented to me with complete sincerity: "American Society is definitely going to be fully automated some day. We know how to live under that condition *without work*. One of the lessons the society can learn from the new community is how to fill up each day, in a meaningful way without work."

The money economy is one of the significant aspects of the machine society under attack by dissenters. In a foray into Wall Street, the citadel of money, the "Protestant ethic," and capitalism, Jerry Rubin, Abbie Hoffman, and some colleagues produced vast shock waves and by demonstration revealed some of the new views of work and money. Rubin describes the experience in *Do It!*:

> The Stock Exchange official looks worried. He says to us, "You can't see the Stock Exchange."
> We're aghast. "Why not?" we ask.

"Because you're hippies and you've come to demonstrate."

"Hippies?" Abbie shouts, outraged at the very suggestion. "We're Jews and we've come to see the stock market."

VISION: *The next day's headlines:* NEW YORK STOCK MARKET BARS JEWS.

We've thrown the official a verbal karate punch. He relents.

The stock market comes to a complete standstill at our entrance at the top of the balcony. The thousands of brokers stop playing Monopoly and applaud us. What a crazy sight for them—longhaired hippies staring down at them.

We throw dollar bills over the ledge. Floating currency fills the air. Like wild animals, the stock brokers climb all over each other to grab the money.

"This is what it's all about, real live money!!! Real dollar bills! People are starving in Biafra!" we shout.

We introduce a little reality into their fantasy lives.

We find ourselves in front of the stock market at high noon. The strangest creeps you ever saw are walking around us: people with short hair, long ties, business suits and brief cases.

They're so serious.

We start dancing "Ring Around the Rosey" in front of the Stock Exchange.

And then we begin burning the things they worship: dollar bills

Straight people start yelling: "Don't! Don't do that!" . . .

Money is a drug. Amerika is a drug culture, a nation of crazy addicts. Money can be used for cigarette paper. Roll a joint. Smoke it.

"What do you do?"

That means: "How do you make your money?" Your work is that thing which produces your money. It defines who you are. Our very consciousness is warped by the green fetish!

Money causes the separation between work and life. People don't do what they dig because they want smelly money. People don't dig what they do because they work for the dollar.

No artist ever did it for the bread. If money motivates you, you're not an artist.

People see each other not as human beings, but as financial transactions. The medium is the message. Money corrupts every human relationship it touches.

Love

One of the major reaction formations of the counterculture is to move toward a more loving, compassionate life style. People are attempting to reverse the process and transform social machines into humanistic groups. The new ethos assumes that the capacity to love exists in all people. "Love is where it's at." A "beautiful person" in the hip world is really a loving person. Drugs are often used to reach a state of love and compassion, even if the emotion is only felt temporarily.

Yet, as in so many other areas of the new life style, there seem to be some discrepancies between the idealized concept of love and the practice of love. A paradoxical example of love on the new scene was expressed in an incident that occurred when I was with some hip people in Big Sur. A hippie high-priest friend of mine pointed out an enormous man with a beard, dressed in hip-style clothes. The fellow, according to my associate, during his lifetime had been on a "heavy criminal assault trip and probably killed a few people." I was told by my friend how he had personally turned the man on to LSD and changed him from "a violent killer to a compassionate, loving person." In the throes of his first beautiful LSD trip his "new partner" told him: "You son-of-a-bitch, I really love you more than I can say. Not in a homo way but really true love. Like, if you ever want anyone killed—you just tell me. That's how much I love you."

VIOLENCE

In the quest for a new humanistic community, violence was for some time eschewed as a methodology for change. It has recently become a vehicle for many rebels who at first reacted negatively against its use. Although violence has since become part of the white counterculture, it has for a long time been a tool used by minority people, especially blacks, to attempt to change the onerous prison of the ghetto. Until the 1960s, however, the aggression and hostility in black ghettos had been primarily confined to people on the same scene. Most homicide and assault in the past occurred in the form of black against black. More recently, with a new pattern of unification, "whitey" and the corrupt system that dehumanizes blacks have been focused upon as the enemy.

Violent behavior for black people, in whatever convoluted form it has taken—from the official condition of slavery to the informal bondage of recent years—has been part of their life style. The minority group struggle has essentially been one of defining themselves as a human entity against the dehumanizing forces imposed by a racist, social machine society. The phases of liberation have included the acceptance of violence imposed by a system of slavery, then a movement into internecine conflict, and more recently the advocacy by some of a direct attack on the oppressive system.

In contrast, white affluent revolutionaries at first responded to their perceived ahuman condition by attempting to produce a super-love community. The love highs of the psychedelic revolution of the 1960s veered into a violent thrust in the late 1960s (especially as a result of the battle of Chicago) and the early 1970s. Abbie Hoffman super-optimistically reviews the transition:

> In the past few years our numbers have grown from hundreds to millions of young people. Our conspiracy has grown more militant. Flower children have lost

their innocence and grown their thorns. We have recognized that our culture in order to survive must be defended. Furthermore we have realized that the revolution is more than digging rock or turning on. The revolution is about coming together in a struggle for change. It is about the destruction of a system based on bosses and competition and the building of a new community based on people and cooperation. That old system is dying all around us and we joyously come out in the streets to dance on its grave. With our free stores, liberated buildings, communes, people's parks, dope, free bodies and our music, we'll build our society in the vacant lots of the old and we'll do it by any means necessary. Right On!

The "by any means necessary" phrase is one that was learned from the bitter struggle of revolutionary blacks in their attempt to overcome the more apparent conditions of a social machine plastic society. In many ways, the newer, affluent, white revolutionaries have learned violence and other strategies from black revolutionaries who for a much longer time have been engaged in both nonviolent and violent patterns for achieving human dignity.

Many white, former flower children decided that they needed to be violent in Chicago and other scenes of the 1960s when the society stereotyped them, because of their beliefs, as "white niggers." In the struggle many have veered off into super-violent behavior directed not necessarily at changing but more precisely at blowing up the social machine society.

A WHITE BOMBER

The metamorphosis of one wealthy, young, counterculture white girl through various phases into the final stage of becoming a bomb-throwing revolutionary is perhaps the most outrageous yet perceptive portrayal of the emergence of violent, affluent, white revolutionaries. In many respects, Diana Oughton's change from a quiet flower child into a bomber is a prototype case similar to that of many other affluent white revolutionaries who have taken the same trip as a reaction formation against a social machine system. The following account is taken from a Pulitzer Prize-winning series of stories by Lucinda Franks and Thomas Powers, distributed by United Press International:

> When Diana Oughton, dead at 28, was buried in Dwight, Illinois, on Tuesday, March 24, 1970, the family and friends gathered at her grave did not really know who she was.
>
> The minister who led the mourners in prayer explained Diana's death as part of the violent history of the times, but the full truth was not so simple.
>
> The newspapers had provided a skeleton of facts. Diana Oughton and two young men were killed March 6 in a bomb explosion which destroyed a townhouse in New York's Greenwich Village. Two young women, their clothes blown off, had run unharmed from the crumbling house and disappeared after showering at the home of a neighbor. It had taken police four days to find Diana's body at the bottom of the rubble and another week to identify it.
>
> Diana and the others were members of the violent revolutionary group known as "the Weathermen." They had turned the townhouse into what police described as a "bomb factory." Months later, they were all to be cited in a grand jury indictment as part of a conspiracy to bomb police, military, and other civic buildings in their campaign to destroy American society.
>
> The facts were clear but the townspeople of Dwight (population 3,086) could not relate them to the Diana they remembered. Her family, too, had their own memories. Diana's father, James Oughton, had watched her tear away from a closely-knit family and a life where beautiful and fine things were important. Her nanny, Ruth Morehart, remembered how un-

easy Diana felt about the money which set the Ough-
tons apart and how, when only six, she had asked:
"Ruthie, why do we have to be rich?"

Carol, her sister, recalled the last phone call, days
before Diana's death, and the voice that asked: "Will
the family stand by me, no matter what?"

Diana's mother, Jane Oughton, wondered whether
her daughter had been making the bomb that killed
her.

There seemed to be many Dianas. There had been
the small-town girl who had grown up with an abun-
dance of good things—a luxurious home, superior
schooling, and people who loved and encouraged her
to be anything in the world she wanted to be. There
had been the frothy, slightly scatterbrained student
at Bryn Mawr College, the self-denying teacher in an
impoverished Guatemalan market town, and finally
the Diana that no one in Dwight really knew or under-
stood—the serious, closely-shorn woman whose mug
shots appeared on police files in at least two cities.

Diana had never stopped loving her family, but the
bomb which accidentally killed her had been designed
ultimately to kill them and their kind. The revolution
she died for would have stripped her father of his vast
farmlands, blown his bank to pieces, and destroyed in
a moment the name and position it had taken a century to build.

Her love of family was not the only traditional value
that Diana was unable to shed. She never lost her gen-
tleness, either, or her sense of morality; but consumed
by revolutionary commitment, she became a terrorist,
fully prepared to live as outlaw and killer.

Diana wanted to destroy many things. Not only
the government she detested but her class, her family,
her past. Perhaps, in the end, even herself.

Diana traveled a path that more or less parallels the trip
of many middle- and upper-class white revolutionaries. They
began with a disenchantment, if not a hostility, toward being
part of what in their view was the "ruling-class." A "ruling-
class" that often indulged its guilt by token-paternalistic char-

ity. They viewed the university as an irrelevant system that no longer had any relationship to the contemporary problems they felt so deeply. They used it (the university) as a staging ground for revolution. In the next phase they joined the flower child psychedelic revolution. Drugs, especially LSD and pot, opened their vistas further to the hypocrisy of their society. When super-love failed to provide the changes they sought, they turned to open encounter—as for example to the Students for a Democratic Society and other such groups. (Diana was a regional director of S.D.S.)

When the forces of "law and order" began to come down heavily on the movement, many went underground. The small extremist group known as the Weathermen began to make bombs to destroy the system when they fully concluded there was no viable way of producing the social change they believed was essential.

It was this strange alchemy of forces that entwined outrageous love with horrendous violence. The starting point for this transition for all of the liberation movements is a motivation for humanistic freedom—in opposition to a social machine. When they conclude that the system is impervious to change, their next logical step is to attempt to destroy it by force.

ROBOPATHIC GAMES

Complete freedom is implied by the expression "do your own thing." This phrase is used repeatedly on the new scene. It ideally refers to being an individual free from the encumbrances, "games," or "hang-ups" of the social machine society. This kind of freedom in the extreme means complete license sexually, politically, and in every other form of behavior. It is the essential battlecry of liberation from the plastic society. The counterculture value orientation is in direct conflict with the superordinate-subordinate people complex that exists in social machine systems.

An important step toward "freedom" in this context is an emancipation from what has been termed "ego games" and what might appropriately in the context of this analysis be called *robopathic games*. A robopathic game in this lexicon is essentially a culturally prescribed act that is institutionalized. It can be anything from a total job situation like the "professor robopathic game" to the "status game" of someone heavily involved with personal prestige. Robopathic ego games are rejected by counterculture people. The goal is to transcend this state of being and to stop being, to the best of one's ability, a "heavy game player."

An extremist statement of this "freedom" from robopathic game playing is defined in *The Psychedelic Experience*, by Timothy Leary, Richard Alpert, and Ralph Metzner. Here, an effort is made to define robopathic "ego games" as they are viewed in the psychedelic world: games are behavioral sequences defined by roles, rules, rituals, goals, strategies, values, language, characteristics, space-time locations, and characteristic patterns of movement. Any behavior not having these nine features is nongame; this includes physiological reflexes, spontaneous play, and transcendental awareness.

There is a recognition that a person cannot be totally removed from some robopathic game-playing; however, the goal is to disengage from this ahuman activity. The cessation of all games is one goal of the psychedelic experience. The elimination of "game-playing" and the death of the (phony) "social ego" are consonant with the drive "to do one's own thing."

Summary

On the surface many of the described reaction-formations to social machines are inchoate and fraught with hypocrisy and chaos. The strategies of violence, nihilism, and anarchy appear to be a strange pattern for achieving a humanistic society. Yet if one looks past the immediate inconsistencies, hypocrisies, and paradoxes of the response, some central themes appear in bold relief. The rebellion of both young and old minority groups and of the affluent drop-outs is against a system of social machines that gives these people in particular a sense of being dehumanized.

The struggle is critical, because this is the first time in history where the forces of annihilation (e.g., ecological destruction, doomsday weaponry, population bomb) may have ultimate consequences. The rebellious patterns are extremist in the sense that they are reaction formations against ahuman elements in the overall social machine system. Many of the patterns and strategies of the counterculture and its reaction-formations have paradoxically become as violent and ahuman-istic as the forces they are attempting to counteract. Yet it should be remembered that the central energy revolves around people's humanistic efforts to extricate themselves and others from becoming or being robopathic game-players in a social machine society.

7

HUMANIZING GROUPS

The control of the robot is complicated for two reasons. One reason is that the robot is man's own creation. He does not meet it face to face, like he did the beasts of the jungle, measuring his strength, intelligence and spontaneity with theirs. The robot comes from within his mind, he gave birth to it. He is confounded like every parent is towards his own child. Rational and irrational factors are mixed therefore in his relationship to robots. In the excitement of creating them he is unaware of the poison which they carry, threatening to kill their own parent. The second reason is that in using robots and zoomatons man unleashes forms of energy and perhaps touches on properties which far surpass his own little world and which belong to the larger, unexplored and

perhaps uncontrollable universe. His task of becoming
a master on such a scale becomes a dubious one as he
may well find himself more and more in the position
of Goethe's Sorcerer's Apprentice who could unleash
the robots but who could not stop them. The Apprentice had forgotten the master's formula, we never had
it. We have to learn this formula and I believe it can
be learned.

—J. L. MORENO

The problems that negatively affect the existential condition
of people in society exist at various levels and can be found in
many degrees of intensity. There are common *miniproblems*
or "little murders" that disturb people's equilibrium. Social
dislocations such as crime, divorce, drug abuse, and even
mental disorders are complex and painful difficulties, but
each carries with it at least a possibility of resolution. The
parameters of these miniproblems are visible and consequently they can often be successfully resolved.

On a more disturbing level of intensity are *megaproblems*,
issues that tend to defy solution because of their enormity.
The presence of robopaths in social machines is an example
of a megaproblem at this ultimate level. One reason why this
condition is so difficult to deal with is that it is not generally
considered bad. It is an existential malaise that inheres in the
"good people" in the system.

Traditionally, social problems or behavior problems are
considered to be manifestations of deviance—acts outside of
the norms, including the law. In this context deviance includes, of course, such patterns as crime, juvenile delinquency, drug addiction, and psychosis. All technological societies are inundated with these problems and the development
of massive therapeutic programs and organizations (often
more dehumanizing than the original problem) is directed at
treating such deviance.

The standard "therapeutic systems" include prisons, mental
hospitals, clinics, and individual treatment. Even the best-
financed, best-staffed, and most efficient of these approaches

fail more than they succeed in treating the *problems* they have been designed to "solve." One reason for their failure is that the treatment programs are artificial efforts to inject deviants with humanistic vitamins they did not receive in the more natural life situations of their families, schools, and communities. Often—as, for example, in prisons—the treatment is worse than the disease, since it compounds the fracture.

The people who are most likely to manifest the symptoms of criminality, drug abuse, mental aberrations, or drop-outism are those people who are asocialized in the most destructive social machines by robopaths. Joey, the "mechanical boy," for example, was very likely a victim of robopathic parents in a social machine family.

Any society that has social problems (or, better, symptom formations) such as alienated, disaffiliated drop-outs, criminals, or drug addicts, is afflicted to the degree of its manifest social problems by a subtle disease in its central nervous system.

The treatment of isolated individuals—the "traditional deviants" who manifest the more overt-apparent problems like criminality and drug abuse—leaves the main societal problem of robopaths in the social machines unaffected. It is the robopaths and their robopathic leaders who perpetrate megaproblem societal diseases. The crimes of pollution, poverty, prejudice, and war, for example, are responsible for more human destruction, physical and social, than all of the traditional deviant social problems (e.g., crime, drug addiction, psychoses) combined. The traditional deviants in this context are the victims of these ills; and the perpetrators (either by commission or omission) are generally in power.

Social problems that demand solutions may thus be divided into two basic categories: (1) "legal deviance," those that are considered "normal" and emanate from official robopathic behavior in social machines; and (2) "traditional deviance," which includes such behavior patterns as crime, drug addiction, and mental illness. Both flow from the same social system.

The "legal deviant" problems of a dehumanized society

are the central focus of this appraisal. If methodologies, strategies, and techniques can be developed for treating robopaths and social machines, the *secondary* symptoms of "traditional deviant" problems would automatically be solved.

The megaproblems of a social machine society defy solution for several reasons. They include situations in which (1) the patients are "self-righteous" about their activities; (2) the patients are in power; (3) their "deviance" is against people, in general, in a superconforming "law and order" context; and (4) the instruments and methodologies for massive social change, short of revolution, are ineffectual or non-existent.

The available counterforces for humanizing groups, in the context of the social machine megaproblems, are about as effective as using a flyswatter to kill a raging lion. Despite the seeming futility of the situation, it is of some usefulness to review the possibilities for positive change.

COUNTERFORCES
FOR HUMANISTIC SOCIAL CHANGE

There are a variety of approaches and vehicles for producing positive social change to counterattack dehumanization and "legal deviance." These approaches and methodologies may be divided into three major categories:

1. *Awareness.* A more coherent and definitive analysis of the forces, issues, and problems of dehumanization is required as a first step for producing a relevant counterattack. Awareness per se can sometimes modify "legal deviant" behavior, because the robopathic perpetrators are in the power position, where they can change their directions. (This area relates to the essential purpose of this book. Nathanael West once commented on this issue: "I believe there is a place for the fellow who yells fire and indicates where some of the smoke is coming from without actually dragging the hose to the spot.")

2. *Spontaneous counterculture movements.* The counter-cultures, militant humanistic social movements, intentional communities, and alternative life styles already in motion may be valuable palliatives for a dehumanized system.
3. *Formal and informal innovation group strategies.* At present there are both incipient and highly developed "innovation group" vehicles for social change that may help resolve some of the problems of dehumanization in social machine societies.

Awareness

As Socrates stated, "the unexamined life is not worth living." One of the characteristics of a humanistic society is continual self-appraisal and self-awareness. Ahuman systems have the effect of sealing people off from each other—to the point where only their images touch. The subtle quality of the dehumanized life is not clearly manifest because it usually contains continuing immediate sensory gratification, very much like the soma pills described by Huxley in *Brave New World.* The worst problem suffered by many robopaths is deadly boredom with themselves and with others. Their existence is not exactly painful, but it is meaningless, irrelevant, and dull. Thoreau described this life style as "leading a life of quiet desperation."

A life of "quiet desperation" is the crude equivalent of a robopathic existence. The surface image of this life style is often shining and sparkling, like the T.V. commercials. The robopathic actors are ostensibly living a full life. Beneath the surface, however, there is deadly boredom, unhappiness, enormous dissatisfaction, and simmering hostility.

It is this pattern of robopathic existence that explains the escalation of youth drop-outism. Most of these youths who have full access to the affluent goals of the society correctly perceive the "victorious" end of the road as the lifeless, robopathic existence led by their parents. They reject the life style carefully planned and made available for them and choose the most outrageous alternatives: communes, dope, poverty, and even violent revolution.

There is increasing evidence of escalating drop-outism from a robopathic existence on the part of the older generation. The traditional escape route from a robopathic existence on the part of executives and of housewives leading lives of quiet desperation in the lap of luxury has been alcoholism and prescribed, legal (unlike their children's illegal) pill-popping. These more traditional patterns are giving way to other forms of adult dropping-out.

A notable example of this situation is found in the rising numbers of men in affluent executive positions who seem to have the "good life" and then quietly disappear into the night. In recent years tens of thousands of men from the upper socioeconomic strata, in top technocratic positions, have disappeared from their robopathic existences into "missing person" status. Some take their families with them (if they are not part of the social machine cause) and others simply drop out on their own.

Unlike these more perceptive and *aware* drop-outs from a robopathic existence, most people locked into their machine work, their bureaucratic role-boxes, and their alienated concern for status-seeking, have limited time or ability to analyze their dilemma. A considerable amount of their time and energy goes into simply defending untenable positions and justifying their frustrating existences.

There are many efforts on the parts of social scientists, writers, and filmmakers to understand the problems of dehumanization. More data, however, are needed about such items as the real extent of people's underlying sense of dehumanization, the true impact of technology and machines on people, and the realities of imminent ecological destruction.

Awareness involves more research evaluation of self, groups, and society. Are people openly and honestly communicating? What social fossils and barnacles have attached themselves to the system? How do people suppress their spirit and their emotions to perform effectively in social machines? How does one segment of the system dominate another (e.g., racism, the oppression of women, etc.)? It is practically impossible to treat a person or a society until there is an admission of pathology and considerable information about the condition. (Interestingly, the most severe political robopaths claim that everything is great.) The beginning of any counterattack on a problem, therefore, is to clarify and properly diagnose the condition, in great detail.

The first step in this awareness, from my viewpoint, is to recognize that our current difficulties are not to be found in the miniproblems of crime, drug abuse, or juvenile delinquency, but in the megaproblem of the dominant social machine society. The robopathic general and others who advocate an "automated battlefield" in "a world wired for death" are much more sinister people than the most deadly sociopathic criminal. Presidential constitutional war crimes are much more deadly than the much-maligned dope-dealer who in effect may be offering immediate relief to suffering, even if the cure has long-term destructive consequences. (In fact, the absurd, unconstitutional Vietnam War has produced as many drug addicts as all of the dope-dealers in the country combined.) The automobile manufacturers of city smog-ovens assault and kill more people each year (even if it happens slowly) than the combined force of all the homicidal muggers and killers who have run amok in this country.

SPONTANEOUS COUNTERCULTURE
MOVEMENTS

In grossly dehumanized societies a majority of the populace are robopaths locked into their special category of social machines. A small minority of the population, many of whom are more *aware* of the malaise, tends to rebel by refusing to play the game and by dropping out or reacting to the various points of the frozen system in nihilistic and extremist fashions. Some of these reaction formations are productive, and others (essentially the violent responses) are at least as destructive as the central problem. Robopathic, violent, and destructive actions are obviously negative forces for combating dehumanization.

Humanistic dissenters, drop-outs, and rebels tend to be viewed by the robocratic power system as a social problem when the rebels are simply calling attention, by their behavior, to the social pathology that exists in the body politic. In this regard they often have the therapeutic impact of producing self-examination and possibly greater awareness on the part of people in the overall power structure.

The dissidents in this context comprise reaction formations against a pathology they notice in the dominant society. This reactive response has generally (although not exclusively) come from younger and more uncommitted members of the society. Many of these disaffiliated people are attempting to develop life styles which are at the opposite end of a continuum from robopathic social machines. If the social machine contains ahuman, loveless, ritualistic, conformist, ruled behavior, the "alienated" reaction formation is a humanistic, loving, extremist form of "doing your own thing." In the extreme, the dissenters have attempted to shift from a controlled-conformist pattern to an anarchistic life style; or from an egocentric self-involvement to a cosmic consciousness that implies ultimate compassion and love.

Many of these uncommitted people have moved into rather far-out conditions of anarchy. In their communal and quasi-communal "do your own thing" setting there is an effort at eliminating all of the rules, structure, and order that are intrinsic parts of the robopath existence.

Along with this increasing number of people disengaging from the dominant society is the proliferation of militant subgroups and anarchistic subcultures. In counterattack against the plastic system the new rebels and revolutionaries say the time and place for anything is Now. College presidents' offices, official meetings, even the halls of Congress are stormed by young people desiring to satisfy and adjust their needs, young people who define their own time and place to demonstrate and use their own rhetoric.

The charge toward super-spontaneity and a rude form of creativity and compassion is often exaggerated to make the point that the natural state of "being" is neglected. Hippies disrobe and make love in public places and present themselves *au natural* in the extreme. The drive for natural states of being pervades segments of the culture striving for what they term freedom and modification of the plastic system.

In their more somber, sober moments, apart from their psychodrama of natural presentations of body, language, sex, and natural functions, people immersed in a revolutionary drive toward tuning back into a more natural state recognize and admit that a measure of cultural definition is useful. Making appointments and arriving on time, vehicles, machines, and schedules have a degree of validity. Their life styles are exaggerated histrionic gestures devoted to super-dramatizing the fact that social machines have gone too far, and in the wrong direction.

The drop-out faction, in attempting to carve out this new life style, emphasizes "doing your own thing" and the lofty goals of being super-loving, breaking one's boundaries, and becoming part of the cosmic unity of nature.

The minority population revolution in this same context is a "by any means" attempt to be free of the oppressive yoke of robopathic racists who have locked them into a box of assumed inferiority. For example, for black people the reaction-formation of "black is beautiful," or, more accurately, black is better, is a reaction formation to centuries of enslaved degradation in positions of abject inferiority. In a very positive way the *intellectual part* of the black revolution has been productive in causing historical, sociological, and psychological self-examination. This process has "therapeutically" enriched the lives of all people in the society.

The black breakout from their dehumanized status in the society has defined a path for other minority groups including

Chicanos, Indians, students, homosexuals, women, and other traditionally oppressed minority categories in technocracies. Many of the strategies of the black revolution have been effectively adapted by these newer groups in the revolution. The establishment has given a considerable amount of attention to drop-outs and revolutionary "deviants." They are considered to be the problem. *A central argument of this book is that in the light of the monstrous social problems of almost suicidal proportions created primarily by the powerful majority—the "well-adjusted," the conservative, and the many robopaths in their midst—the majority, not the minority, is the problem.*

It is the robopathic majority that produces absurd unsolvable wars from which they cannot retreat, and deadly air pollution. It is their impact on the more sensitive people around them that escalates psychosis (escape from social machine pressure) among people who are more responsive to these ahuman pressures.

There is an increasing emancipation from slave roles by black, white, red, young, old, "gay," and female persons who have in some measure broken out of their positions of inferiority and slavery imposed by the dehumanizing social machines of the plastic society.

A result of the screeching rhetoric and dialogue is that many young hip drop-outs and revolutionaries have in some cases "turned on" their "square" or "Uncle Tom" parents to a more fulfilling life style. Integral robopathic role-players in technocratic systems have increasingly examined their hole card, since they have *had* to encounter the dissenters in their own families and communities. The revolutionaries by their practice of putting down what they could easily acquire—the positions of affluence and power in the plastic society—have forced a degree of awareness and self-examination on the part of such robopathic role-players as professors, judges, politicians, and businessmen. In this regard they have had some influence in making the system more humanistic.

In other respects some of the experimental life styles of

the revolutionaries have broken ground for a more humanistic way of life. A greater sexual awareness and openness in tech niques of making love has turned on many people in the overall society. (This may, in part, account for the enormous interest in the "sensuous" how-to-do-it books that now flood the market.)

Drug use, with all of its negative consequences and perilous experimentation, has opened up many people so that they see the world around them with different eyes. In general, the dissenters—with their super-emphasis on loving, touching, living closer to nature, seeing more cosmic realities, being more spontaneous and creative in human interaction, living more in the "here and now" than in the past—have helped to focus the problem and provide a greater awareness of humanistic qualities. This greater awareness and the alternative life styles have been instrumental in producing some humanistic social change.

Robopaths in Eden

The emphasis so far has been on the more positive aspects of the counterculture. It must be noted that revolutionaries and dissidents are *also* capable of producing and participating in social machines. In the revolution there are many robopathic hippies, yippies, and minority group militants who get locked in to hypocritical, ahuman, acompassionate, nihilistic positions and destroy more than they create. This is obvious in the action of those revolutionaries who have actually killed people. In trying to destroy the plastic beast they have themselves adopted its violent and dehumanized patterns.

In another context many of the alternative, experimental life styles developed in the new community have been ineffectual and hypocritical efforts. The communal way of life, for example, seems to have dominantly been a failure. My personal empirical studies of the alternative life-style communes over the past several years (rural and urban) have revealed some glaring problems that contradict some of the glowing

underground newspaper and even mass media reports. Inherent in the commune scene are many of the problems that
plague many middle- and upper-class young people attempting
to work out alternative life styles. The communal movement
may serve as a revealing microcosm for examining the overall
counterculture movement and its own robopathic social
machine tendencies.

A return to the land and a natural environment by hip
people "turned on" to nature is an admirable and adventure-
some goal. However, the quick switch for city dwellers to this
new way of life seems beset with complicated problems.

A central one is the hip view of leadership. No one seems to
want any heavy authority telling him what to do. In fact,
part of the reason for being on the scene is to escape leaders
and structures of government. Yet the avoidance of this natural law of human organization related to the natural need for
leader roles often defeats the possibility of a successful
community.

Since The Beginning, according to all recorded history, a
select few in any tribe have assumed power and decision-
making functions. The ignorance of this necessity by potential counterculture "leaders" and "followers" has produced chaos and mass confusion in the communes that I have
seen.

Noncompassionate, physically strong or violent people
(Charles Manson is a prototype) often fill the leadership
vacuum and take over when there is "loving anarchy." The
hippie assumption, that when "everyone does their own thing"
order will prevail, does not seem to work. Sometimes sociopaths (not robopaths) in the group, who have a thin veneer of
"love" on the surface, begin to take advantage and manipulate
people for their own egocentric ends.

Another difficult problem seems to be the socialization of
children. With all the "cleanups" and rationalizations about
being in a more natural environment, children grow up better
with some definition of order rather than in the typical alternate society conditions of almost total anarchy and chaos.

Children desire reasonable boundaries that can give meaning and style to their lives.

Parents in the new communities are admittedly escaping a preordained robopathic existence, and are engaged in an intense search for identity and religious experience. This totally time-consuming effort that characterizes the hip community places children, in many cases, in an abandoned position. People freaked out or even mildly loaded on drugs are not sufficiently stable to teach children what they need to know about life. Stoned people (either by alcohol or drugs) are generally too egocentric, self-involved, and unstable to "give" to children—even though their self-concept is to believe they are doing fine.

An even more debatable practice that often occurs in communes that are drug-oriented is the giving of drugs to children.

A dominant characteristic of the new scene is a screeching counterextremism. The experimenters attempt to go from overorganization in a social machine to no organization; from alienation and loneliness to complete cohesion in a group; from self to cosmic consciousness (with drugs); from no emotional feeling to complete and all-encompassing experience.

My overall view of these experiments with alternative lifestyles is mixed. Counterattack is a useful endeavor against a suicidal plastic society; however, a more moderate reaction seems to be a more productive mode of response than extremism.

Even though I recognize many positive characteristics in the counterculture, my view of its potential for "greening" social machine societies is more pessimistic and cynical than the perspective of others. A dedicated and widely read advocate of the curative power of the counterculture is Charles Reich, who in his *The Greening of America* is most optimistic about salvation emerging from young people and from the elite counterculture.

One problem with Reich's extravagant faith is that most young people in this country are socialized in social machine families, and this majority will most likely occupy roles in the factories of the machine society. Very few young people will occupy the ivory towers of Yale and Harvard where Reich collected most of his information about potential social change and *Consciousness III*.

Reich's sample of young Yale students who will green America is a small and unique group of people. These are young people who, in effect, by virtue of their families, are the new aristocrats, supported by the labor of millions of machine-enslaved robopaths.

The turned-on hippies gamboling in the grass are Reich's heroes and models for a grooving *Consciousness III* society. Unfortunately, the achievements of advocates of extremism are too often entwined with the fruits of the "death-dealing machine." Their affluent, robopathic families frequently support their drop-outism, drug purchases, and communal life style. Some people, somewhere, have to grow the food, harvest the crops, and manufacture the clothes and some of the controlled machines that society requires. Too many of Reich's green young people are too remote from the realities of *real work* to produce meaningful social change.

Most of them, like the hero of Erich Segal's (Reich's literary counterpart at Yale) *Love Story*, have to return to sneak some spiritual and financial guidance from their rich (robopathic) fathers when the chips are down. (The father in *Love Story* whose position is attacked by the son's modest drop-outism breathes a sigh of relief when the prodigal son returns for materialistic succoring and the symbolic correctness of his robopathic existence is reconfirmed.)

I agree that the dissent and new life styles have been somewhat helpful as counterpoints to the machine society; however, it should be noted that the revolutionaries are in fact a small minority that are relatively powerless in the total scheme of technological systems. Unfortunately, the affluent hippie minority will not provide, as Reich seems to think and others desperately want to believe, the final counterforce to the social machine.

The minority group revolutions (black, brown, red, others) have also unfortunately had a modest impact, in the face of powerful laws and customs that perpetuate the status enslavement of these groups. Here, too, the movement has had some influence on the plastic society in terms of enlightenment about the problems of oppression, some legislative changes, minority group pride in heritage, and greater job opportunities. Relatively speaking, however, the plastic society maintains the dehumanizing status quo, despite these hopeful counterforces and counterattacks.

In brief, it is my opinion that the variety of countercultures and revolutionary efforts have been useful in focusing on the problem of social machines; however, their longevity, sustaining power, and real impact has been modest. In overview, their immediate future potential for defeating the plastic system is slight. If real social change is to come it must take place in the heart of the matter. Change may be produced if the robopaths themselves become aware of the nature of social machines and help to develop new techniques for counterattacking the problem inside the dehumanized societal system.

FORMAL AND INFORMAL
INNOVATION GROUP METHODS AND STRATEGIES

SENSITIVITY TRAINING FOR U.S. BUREAUCRATS

Washington—The Federal Government is flirting with the far-out field of sensitivity training.

Several departments are running employees through short-term courses in an effort to make them more sympathetic to people than paper work.

A few advocates of the movement see it as a tool that could humanize the faceless governmental machine. They've been calling in sensitivity coaches for problems ranging from racism to slow-moving memos.

But the government's approach so far has been pretty tame. None of the bureaucrats are crawling around under blankets, taking off their clothes or baring their soul. Mostly they just talk. . . . All of it is

an outgrowth of the "human potentials" movement
which focuses on the idea that man's latent resources
can be tapped through exploring his relationships
with others.

It is well to repeat here at the outset that most currently
available methods for the social change of megaproblems are
in the "flyswatter" category; yet it seems necessary to begin
somewhere, with some leverage for change that is immediately
visible.

In the dominant technological system, although humanistic
aspiration and motivations are boxed in, there exists some
potential for developing a more humanistic system. The possibility for change operates on the premise that the most de-
vout robopath, locked into the most deadly social machine,
has the potential for becoming a loving, compassionate person. These small innovation group approaches could, in time,
hopefully convert social machines into humanistic groups.
(This extravagant faith used to become actualized in the
Frank Capra-Jimmy Stewart movies of the 1930s when the
hard-hearted bureaucrats and politicians at the end of the
movie would become super-humanists; and everyone, rich
and poor alike, would go off together into the sunshine of a
new life. The simple, possible loving solutions of the 1930s
may in part account for the nostalgia of people in the 1970s
for that era.)

The formal system has produced a variety of group techniques for cracking through the defensive shields of robopathic
game-players. In the past decade a variety of such humanistic
systems has become popular for producing changes in robopaths in social machines. These approaches, generally referred
to as group therapy, include such specific methods as sensitivity training, psychodrama, Synanon, encounter techniques,
and Gestalt therapy. A central theme of all of these approaches is to produce interaction situations (for brief and
sometimes long periods of time) where people communicate
on a deep humanistic level. The ideal premise or goal is that
this type of interaction will produce greater self-awareness,

better ability to communicate, get people more in touch with their "real feelings," resolve identity problems, increase spontaneity and creativity, and in general make people more humanistic in their interpersonal relationships. The overall impact would be to humanize groups. In this regard, J. L. Moreno comments: "A truly therapeutic procedure cannot have less an objective than the whole of mankind."

These varied approaches are what I would term "innovation groups" in the sense that the normative factors of interaction in the standard society are modified. Innovative attitudes toward time, space, roles, verbal volume, and language are adopted in order to help people communicate with each other on a deeper, more meaningful level of interaction. The rules of formal, routine interaction are dramatically changed in these groups so that new approaches, feelings, and experiences are permitted. This possibility attempts to open people and groups to "changes."

The central conscious and unconscious goal of all of these approaches is to get people to become better at humanistic interaction—to modify robopathic role-players so that they communicate better with themselves (their interior feelings) and with other people. To help people establish their personal identities so that they can become more compassionate members and participants in the larger humanistic community.

The new approaches in part supplant older styles of "individual treatment" that have too often become calcified social machines of the plastic society. Psychoanalysis, for example, has become an antique form of treatment, at least for combating robopathic behavior in social machines. Classical psychoanalysts are too often robopaths themselves in the sense that they play *super-ordinate* roles with *subordinate* patients. The emphasis is on methodology, not on touching, relating, or human compassion. The analysand is often further isolated from his social groups in the process. The procedure of analysis is past-oriented rather than geared to the "here and now." The two participants, analyst and analysand, are forced to function in an ahuman format. One person, the psychoanalyst, is seated and methodologically denies his feelings, while the other, the patient, is seated or reclined and cannot get up and act out when he feels like it. The description and analysis here is of the general structure of the traditional therapeutic situation. Obviously there are many individual psychotherapists whose humanistic insights allow them to transcend the limitations of their profession. Increasingly, many sensitive therapists are turning to group methodologies as adjuncts to or replacements for their individual practices.

Group methodologies seem better suited than individual approaches for combating robopathic phenomena. From an institutional point of view, many "helping" organizations have become more humanistic as they have attempted to treat the symptoms of the plastic society. In medicine and in efforts to control drug abuse, for example, the Haight-Ashbury Free Medical Clinic, founded by Dr. David Smith, has pioneered a new approach to medical care. Similarly, Dr. Joel Fort has helped develop a center that seeks to solve a variety of social problems. Both clinics are largely run by "patients" and volunteers (professionals and laymen) from the community. These organizations seem to be beneficial to thousands of participants from all walks of life.

SYNANON

In this general humanistic direction, Synanon, founded by Charles E. Dederich in 1958, has set a brilliant and significant example for many other carbon-copy organizations that are now emerging around the world. Unlike many of the other group approaches which are essentially part-time activities, Synanon encompasses many of these methodologies in a round-the-clock "live-in" social system.

Synanon is an "intentional community" that has proven useful in its brief history for counterattacking many of the consequences of social machines. The organization at the outset was devoted to extricating alcoholics and drug addicts from their self-destructive patterns. Its scope has since been enlarged and it has become a community geared to providing an alternative life style for people (many without apparent traditional symptoms) from all walks of life who are dissatisfied with their existence in the larger society.

The Synanon community and program includes an encounter form of group therapy, an approach to racial integration, a solution for some facets of bureaucratic organization, a different way of being religious, an unusual kind of communication, and a novel approach to the cultural arts and philosophy. One side effect of intense involvement is that the participants (many of whom were criminal addicts) have found what they consider to be a superior life style. Many people who have never been "deviants" in the illegal sense have involved themselves in the Synanon program to escape from social machines and from their former robopathic life patterns.

PSYCHODRAMA: PHILOSOPHY AND METHODOLOGY

Psychodrama is a philosophical and methodological approach to human interaction. It was specifically designed by its originator J. L. Moreno (in 1911) to combat the forces of robopathology and social machines. The psychodramatic system has been the fountainhead for many of the innovation group approaches that have been developed over the past fifty years. Psychodrama's *methodology* and *philosophy* will be assessed here in depth, since they help to explain the structure of other innovation group approaches to the fundamental problems of a plastic society.

Psychodrama has considerable adaptability and flexibility. All that is required for a session is the problem (philosophical or concrete), the group, and a psychodramatist. The freedom for a group to act out its problems is represented by the freedom of space of a stage, or any open space. In this regard, psychodrama "on stage" is an intensified version of people's lives on the more formal "stage" of society.

In a session a *subject* emerges from the group with a particular problem to be explored. It may be his relationship to his parents, his job, or, more generally, his existential-spiritual condition. The subject or protagonist is a representative of the group (the immediate group present and the one in the larger society). All participants in the group are encouraged to enact their emotions and conflicts through the subject.

The following actual session may serve as an example of a group psychodrama. Out of a group of eighteen people a man steps forward on the stage. He says that he has all the accouterments of success. He has professional stature, likes his job, earns a sizeable income, claims to love and be loved by his wife and children; however, there is a void in his life. He cannot specify what it is, but he feels empty and unfulfilled; and he sees no prospects for positive change. Life has no meaning for him. He has recently been contemplating suicide; as he put it, he wants "to get out of the nothingness of this life."

The session specifically opens on a make-believe Long Island commuter train in a scene where the man is returning from a day at work as an executive in a large corporation in Manhattan. "I feel as if I'm on a train that is on a track that will never end. And if it does, I don't want to get off."

In the three-hour session, he plays himself in his most relevant relationships, with his family, at work, and with the memory and reality of his dead parents, who wanted him to succeed in a specific way. As he explores his inner world by objectifying it in actuality on the stage, he begins to make a series of discoveries.

He is not as honest in his human relations as he overtly claims or likes to think. He "repeats and repeats and repeats" the same behavior "day after day after day." He has lost the memory of any peak experiences in his life; for example, his romance with his wife, the early happy years of their marriage, the birth of his son. His job has become for him an empty ritual, it no longer has any point—if it ever did.

In the psychodrama of his robopathic existence he tries radical new alternatives to his life: an emotional scene reviving his marriage; a really honest discussion with his son; a scene denouncing himself and his fellow (robopathic) employees. His spontaneity and creativity become revived by the session. He renews his interest in his social sphere of people. He literally cries about his not touching or feeling the people close to him anymore. He does this psychodramatically and begins to revive his humanistic juices.

The members of the group join in on the session and begin to reveal their points of identification with the protagonist. The protagonist and the group in the "psychodrama of robopathic existence" experience each other in new, different, and creative ways. They touch, hug, cry, examine, speculate—in brief, they live a deeper, more humanistic reality. Most important, the spontaneity and creativity they have experienced carries over into their "real life." The session has revived some creative forces in the man that open him up further to his family, friends, and colleagues when he leaves the psychodrama session. This revival hopefully produces larger ripples of impact.

Psychodrama is primarily a group process, although it may shift from the group to an individual's problem at varying points in a session. The director constantly moves toward mobilizing the group to work together on their mutual problems and feelings, even though only one or two members of the group serve as the session's primary representatives. The response of people in the audience is often greater than that of people on stage. There are several central elements, roles, and techniques used in psychodrama to focus a session. These are described in detail in the following sections in order to emphasize the dynamics of psychodrama, and also to point to possible applications of these techniques as ways of humanizing the larger "stage" of life.

The Director

The role of the director continually fluctuates in the course of psychodrama sessions. The director may be passive or aggressive, depending on the needs of the subject and the group. At times the director may play the needed role of an authoritarian father or a demanding mother, when he feels he can perform the role more effectively than an auxiliary ego. The director observes nonverbal as well as verbal communications. For example, a protagonist may be overtly agreeing quite pleasantly with his employer; at the same time his red, clenched fists reveal an underlying hostility that may be manifestly related to the subject of the session.

In the broader life scene, some people become directors by helping to open up people close to them—by "directing" them to examine their deeper feelings. Such individuals facilitate more honest and compassionate human interaction. An example would be a colleague who goes beyond his or her formal role in order to relate to someone at a personal level.

Role-reversal Technique

Role-reversal is the psychodramatic procedure in which A becomes B and B becomes A. For example the executive subject in the briefly described existential psychodrama takes the role of his wife and the woman playing the role of his wife becomes him. This provides him with another refreshing perspective on his life. He sees himself through his wife's eyes. As the wife, the subject said in the psychodrama of their sex life: "You've become a complete bore. You never do anything new or different. Screwing you is like being in bed with a machine." Role-reversal is used for any or all of the following purposes in a session:

1. The subject who plays the role of the relevant other—as, for example, the husband becoming the wife—often begins to feel and better understand the other person's position and reactions in the situation. This tends to improve their sensitivity, compassion, and empathy. For example, in the session described, the father reverses roles with his six-year-old son. In the role of the son he begins to feel what it is like to look at himself as a father, and at the world from a six-year-old

viewpoint. The father in the role of the son says: "Dad, you're always so busy. You never read to me or hug and kiss me anymore. What's wrong with me?" (Often at this point the father is put back in his own role by a role-reversal and must respond to his son's poignant and pertinent question.)

2. Role-reversal may be used to help the protagonist see himself as if in a mirror. The father playing the role of his son sees himself through the child's perception. This instrument has the effect of producing insights for the protagonist as he sees himself through the eyes of another.

3. Role-reversal is often effective in augmenting the spontaneity of the protagonist, by shifting him out of robot-like defenses. The subjects may become more creative in their real life roles by shifting themselves out of their usual ruts of standard enactments in psychodrama. Since the session is in part play-acting, without the real adversary, the subject can try out new responses of anger, love, or undestanding. This broadens the person's repertoire in real life. Also, the subject has an opportunity to assess the depth of his feelings.

For example, in the described session we learned that the executive had tremendous hostility for his father, even though he was dead. After literally being in his father's shoes in a psychodramatic role-reversal, the subject began to understand what his father went through in his life, and he became more sympathetic to his position. In the session he "forgave" his father, and in the process he released part of his gut-like ball of hostility.

Role-reversal is not only a technique; it can also become part of a person's life style. To take the role of others is in reality to become more sympathetic and compassionate. Knowing more about how the other person feels is bound to affect one's everyday actions in a positive way.

The Double

The double gets behind the subject and takes the subject's role. The double can give the protagonist needed support in a situation. At other times the double may express feelings of

184

fear, hostility, or love which the protagonist, on his own, is unable to act out.

As an example, the father in the case cited had a double who began to say (for him) to his child, "You take up too much of my time, even when I'm not with you. You interfere with my success in life. I'm forced to keep a job I hate just to support you and your mother." After the father released his hostility by confirming what the double had expressed for him, he claimed to feel better.

The double may take a chance and express certain hypotheses which appear in the situation. For example, a double in the case cited earlier said (for the subject) to his wife, "I hate you because you're just like my mother." The subject may confirm or deny the double's statement. The subject may or may not agree with many thoughts which the double expresses. In this respect, the double is useful in helping the subject elicit new cues or lines of further understanding. The double produces an added dimension of the subject which he, for various reasons, cannot present or examine himself. The double thus helps the subject to enlarge his spontaneous role-playing ability.

Here again the technique illustrates a real-life necessity for people—a need to identify more intensively with others. Doubling in real life opens up new and different lines of communication and interaction among people.

The Soliloquy

The soliloquy is a technique that parallels, for example, Hamlet's soliloquy in Shakespeare's play. It involves the subject thinking his thoughts out loud in the middle of action, in an important life situation. It is a useful technique for expressing the hidden thoughts and action tendencies of the protagonist in a situation. The protagonist's improvisations are parallel with his overt actions and thoughts and with hidden action tendencies and thoughts which he may have in reference to a specific person or a specific situation. When the protagonist soliloquizes, he may clarify and structure insights and perceptions, and prepare himself for future situations. The degree that a person's soliloquy differs from his behavior in a situation is the degree to which he is presenting a false image to the world. This is one of the essential problems of a robopathic existence.

A robopathic person's inner, buried emotions and yearnings may be revealed in the soliloquy by a double, and this may facilitate more humanistic behavior. In regular interaction, more honest soliloquies encourage people to present their most truthful feelings in action. In the "robopathic existence" session, when it was learned that the man involved had considerable hostility toward his father, he was encouraged to actually express it by punching a pillow held by an auxiliary ego playing the dead father's role. After a furious barrage of hostile punches that had been pent up for years, the director asked the protagonist to stop after each additional punch and talk about it. After each punch the director asked, "What was that for?" The subject in various ways stated that he felt rejected, abused, abandoned by his father. Honestly releasing these feelings for the first time in his life made him feel better.

In later discussion with the group the executive learned he was not alone. Many members of the group felt estranged in the same way. This group confessional made many people in the group, who had shared their inner emotions, feel better. The total impact on the protagonist who acted out was both emotional and intellectual; and the overall group had a greater feeling of being together and more loving with each other.

Moreno comments succinctly on the relationship between action and the intellect:

> Excessive insight often hinders spontaneity from flourishing and the striving toward self-actualization. It is a tragedy. Frequently we turn toward the intellect and are often carried away by a false sense of euphoria, losing contact with the here and now, the immediate

task of our responsibility. On the other hand, when we turn away from the intellect, we lose the great sense of meaning and value which we would want to attach to an action. And so we are faced with two extremes: the simpleminded, naive, unsophisticated hero and the excessive, overbearing, paralyzed nondoer.

Frozen robopathic non-doers are often spurred into action and awareness by psychodrama. Sometimes an element of overreacting is encouraged. The psychodramatic session may have characteristics of what Moreno calls "surplus reality." The situation is blown up out of proportion and magnified to enable the subject and the group to get a closer look at the situation under the psychodramatic microscope. The subject and the group get to see themselves with all of their facades in a setting in which errors of judgment and behavior are not as destructive or traumatic as they might be in the real situation. These surplus-reality explorations give people an opportunity to be more inventive in their human relationships. People in the group are encouraged to become freer, more spontaneous, and more humanistic in their real life.

In this regard Moreno advocates a more universal psychodrama, a psychodrama of the streets in real human situations:

> Psychodrama is not restricted to a psychodrama theatre. Life may provoke a simple man to turn psychodramatist. Imagine that you are in a restaurant eating at a table and a Negro sits down next to you. The manager comes and advises him to leave: "Negroes are not allowed as guests." You may have the urge to put yourself in the place of the Negro and, in protest, when he leaves the restaurant, you leave with him. This is the first psychodramatic law: Put yourself into the place of a victim of injustice and share his hurt. Reverse roles with him.
>
> You may remember the concentration camps in Auschwitz. Millions of Jews have been thrown into gas chambers and burned alive. Men, women, chil-

dren. Millions of people knew about it, Germans and non-Germans, but did nothing. But there emerged during that period of the lowest depth of inhumanity a few men who dared to challenge this action, this mass murder. They were a number of German pastors who insisted on going with the Jewish victims into the camps to suffer with them every kind of humiliation, starvation, brutality, even going into the gas chambers to be burned alive. Against the proudest of the Nazi authorities they felt their responsibility to participate with the innocent victims in the same martyrdom. And when they were not permitted to go, they were shot and died. Among such unusual characters in Auschwitz were three men—a priest named Kolbe, another priest by the name of Lichtenberg, and another who was officially a Nazi storm trooper by the name of Gerstein. These men died as bearers of truth.

A bearer of truth is not necessarily the instrument of a godhead or of any particular religion, although he may be related to a particular religion (as in the case of the Christian). The bearer of truth does what he does because of his innermost desire to establish the truth and justice and love of humanity regardless of consequences. It is a moral imperative.

In this regard psychodrama and other spontaneous methods have a broad applicability and hopeful potential for humanizing groups. By means of these systems people are encouraged to break out of their circumscribed robopathic roles, to communicate, to express their deeper emotional feelings, and to become more compassionate.

The growing revolutionary attack against dehumanized societies can have the effect, up to a point, of making people aware of ahuman conditions and of providing some sketchy experimental methods for a counterattack that would utilize the described innovation group approaches. One caveat is required in this regard. Innovation group methods are at best only crutches—auxiliary or substitute approaches for modifying social machines and producing significant social change.

The basic institutions of a social machine society need to be changed in order to produce a fundamental revitalization of regular, day-to-day human interaction.

A reversal of the machine systems' social death-dealing consequences requires an effort at all levels, by all people in a social machine society. The first step is an awareness and an acceptance of the fact that the times are precarious. There is no external enemy to be confronted—it exists in dialectical battle in all people, and in all societies. No one, not even the most horrendous political robopath, should be "put down." The condition of robopathic social death is the real enemy.

Creative and more humanistic qualities are required in the basic institutional forms of the family, education, religion, economics, and government if overall social machine systems are to be significantly modified. A greater consciousness of the megaproblem of robopaths versus social machines will hopefully activate people in various positions in plastic societies to move toward vitally needed humanistic social change.

NOTES

PAGE	LINE	
8	22	J. L. Moreno, *Psychodrama*, vol. I, 3rd ed. (Beacon, N.Y.: Beacon House, 1970), pp. 92–93.
11	6	Albert Camus, *The Rebel*, trans. Anthony Bower (New York: Vintage Books, 1956), pp. 279–80.
	29	*Hard Contract*, written and directed by S. Lee Pogostin (Twentieth Century-Fox).
25	10	San Francisco *Sunday Examiner and Chronicle*, December 27, 1970.
27	1	Stanley Milgram, "Some Conditions of Obedience and Disobedience to Authority, *Human Relations* 18 (1965): 57–75. See also Stanley Milgram, "Behavioral Study of Obedience," *J. abnorm. soc. Psychol.* 67 (1963): 371–78.
30	19	Nathanael West, *The Day of the Locust* (New York: New Directions, 1963), p. 74.

2   *The Emergence of Robopathology and Related Syndromes*

34	1	New York *Times*, December 14, 1969.
35	3	As quoted by Tom Tiede, *Calley: Soldier or Killer?* (New York: Pinnacle Books, 1971), pp. 38–40.
	34	Ibid., p. 16.
36	2	Ibid.
	9	Julian Wilson and James M. Smith, "The Battle Hymn of Lt. Calley" (Nashville, Tennessee: Shelby Singleton Music, Inc./Quickit Publishing Co., 1971).
	31	As quoted by Tiede, *Calley: Soldier or Killer?*, p. 51.

PAGE	LINE	
37	13	Abraham Maslow, "Psychological Data and Value Theory," in *New Knowledge in Human Values*, ed. Maslow (New York: Harper, 1959), p. 127.
41	7	Charles E. Silberman, *Crisis in the Classroom* (New York: Random House, 1970), pp. 207–8.
	30	J. L. Moreno, *Theater of Spontaneity* (Beacon, N.Y.: Beacon House, 1947), pp. 105–6.
43	26	For a more extensive discussion of this issue see Lewis Yablonsky, *The Hippie Trip* (New York: Pegasus, 1968).
44	15	Bruno Bettelheim, *The Informed Heart* (Glencoe, Ill.: Free Press, 1960), pp. 58–59.
	27	Bruno Bettelheim, "Joey: A 'Mechanical Boy,'" *Scientific American* (March, 1959): 116–27.
47	32	Paul Tappan, *Crime, Justice and Correction* (New York: McGraw-Hill, 1960), p. 137.
48	1	Harrison Gough, "A Sociological Theory of Psychopathy," *American Journal of Sociology* (March, 1948): 360.
	14	Arthur Rabin, "Psychopathic (Sociopathic) Personalities," in *Legal and Criminal Psychology*, ed. Hans Toch (New York: Holt, Rinehart & Winston, 1961), p. 278.
49	17	G. H. Mead, *Mind, Self and Society* (Chicago: University of Chicago Press, 1934), p. 142.
	26	Harry Stack Sullivan, *Conceptions of Modern Psychiatry*, 2nd ed. (New York: Norton, 1953), p. 24.
50	2	Lewis Yablonsky, *The Violent Gang* (New York: Macmillan, 1962).
51	3	Ibid., p. 198.

3   *Selected Observations on Technocracy and Dehumanization*

PAGE	LINE	
		(New York: Harcourt, Brace & World, 1934), p. 16.
63	27	Georg Simmel, "The Metropolis and Mental Life," in *The Sociology of Georg Simmel*, ed. and trans. Kurt H. Wolff (Glencoe, Ill.: Free Press, 1950), p. 413.
64	4	Fyodor Dostoyevsky, *Notes from Underground; Poor People; The Friend of the Family: Three Short Novels by Fyodor Dostoyevsky*, trans. Constance Garnett (New York: Dell, 1960), p. 45.
66	4	Ernest van den Haag, "Of Happiness and Despair We Have No Measure," in *Mass Culture: The Popular Arts in America*, ed. Bernard Rosenberg and David White (Glencoe, Ill.: Free Press, 1957), p. 446.
67	34	Robert K. Merton, *Mass Persuasion: The Social Psychology of a War Bond Drive* (New York: Harper, 1946), p. 142.
68	14	C. Wright Mills, *The Power Elite* (New York: Oxford University Press, 1956), p. 314.
	32	Ibid., p. 320.
69	7	Ibid., pp. 320–21.
	25	The concept of bureaucracy was first presented and closely analyzed by the German sociologist Max Weber. A more contemporary sociologist, Robert K. Merton, has contributed importantly to the understanding of this concept. Much of the present discussion rests on and is paraphrased from the insightful observations on bureaucracy in Robert K. Merton's classic volume, *Social Theory and Social Structure* (Glencoe, Ill.: Free Press, 1957), pp. 195–206.
71	23	*Joe*, screenplay by Norman Wexler (New York: Avon, 1970), p. 62.

PAGE	LINE	
72	5	Robert K. Merton, *Social Theory and Social Structure*, pp. 199–200.
	22	Santa Monica *Evening Outlook*, August 18, 1969.
73	31	Robert K. Merton, *Social Theory and Social Structure*, pp. 200–201.
74	9	Ibid., p. 201.
	28	Alan Harrington, *Life in the Crystal Palace* (New York: Knopf, 1958), pp. 86–87.
76	3	Franz Kafka, *The Trial*, trans. Edwin and Willa Muir (New York: Random House, Modern Library, 1956), pp. 5–6, 7, and 9–10.
77	31	Erich Fromm, *The Sane Society* (New York: Fawcett World Library, 1955), pp. 114–15.
78	7	Susanne Langer, *Philosophy in a New Key* (New York: New American Library Mentor Books, 1956), p. 226.
79	14	Theodore Roszak, *The Making of a Counter Culture* (Garden City, N.Y.: Doubleday Anchor Books, 1969), p. xiii.
	31	Some of this section on alienation is based on and paraphrased from Melvin Seeman's penetrating article, "On the Meaning of Alienation," *American Sociological Review* 24 (December, 1959): 783–91.
81	22	Alvin Toffler, *Future Shock* (New York: Random House, 1970).
82	15	Arthur Miller, *Death of a Salesman* (New York: Viking, 1949), act II, p. 98.
	21	Roy Haynes, Los Angeles *Times*, October 1, 1969.
83	15	New York *Herald Tribune*, November 2, 1961.
	18	Émile Durkheim, "The Anomic Division of

PAGE	LINE	
		Labor," in *The Division of Labor in Society*, trans. George Simpson (Glencoe, Ill.: Free Press, 1933), pp. 364–73.
	31	Robert K. Merton, *Social Theory and Social Structure*, p. 162.
84	8	Erving Goffman, "Alienation from Interaction," in *Interaction Ritual: Essays on Face-to-Face Behavior* (Chicago: Aldine, 1967), pp. 113–36.
	14	Ibid., p. 136.
85	14	Albert Camus, *The Stranger*, trans. Stuart Gilbert (New York: Vintage Books, 1946), pp. 83–84.
86	15	Ibid., pp. 111 and 121.
87	18	Erich Fromm, *The Sane Society*, p. 111.
	34	Karen Horney, *Neurosis and Human Growth: The Struggle Toward Self-Realization* (New York: Norton, 1950), p. 157.
88	4	Erich Fromm, *The Sane Society*, p. 111.
	20	Erich Fromm, "Two Aspects of Freedom for Modern Man," in *Escape from Freedom* (New York: Rinehart, 1941), pp. 103–35.
	31	Erich Fromm, *The Revolution of Hope* (New York: Harper & Row, 1968), p. 2.
89	8	José Ortega y Gasset, *The Revolt of the Masses*, authorized translation (New York: Norton, 1932), p. 18.

4 In Social Machines

94	21	David Riesman, Nathan Glazer, and Reuel Denny, *The Lonely Crowd* (New York: Doubleday Anchor Books, 1953), p. 66.
96	10	See Joe McGinnis, *The Selling of a President, 1968* (New York: Trident, 1969).

PAGE	LINE	
97	17	Charles Horton Cooley, *Social Organization* (New York: Scribner, 1929), pp. 23–24.
103	15	United Press International; in San Francisco *Chronicle,* November 25, 1970.

5   *Reaction Formations*

113	1	William O. Douglas, *Points of Rebellion* (New York: Random House, 1969), p. 96.
114	31	Georg Simmel, "The Stranger," in *The Sociology of Georg Simmel*, pp. 404–5.
116	2	Charles Reich, *The Greening of America* (New York: Random House, 1970).
	24	Ibid., p. 2.
118	17	William O. Douglas, *Points of Rebellion*, p. 9.
	24	Ibid., p. 10.
119	25	Peter L. and Brigitte Berger, "The Blueing of America," *New Republic* (April 3, 1971): 20–23.
120	14	Jerry Rubin, *Do It!* (New York: Simon & Schuster, 1970), p. 86.
121	1	Ibid., p. 132.
	10	Abbie Hoffman, *Revolution for the Hell of It* (New York: Dial Press, 1968), p. 157.
	19	Jerry Rubin, *Do It!*, pp. 146–47.
122	3	Ibid., p. 12.
	17	Ibid., pp. 93–96.
123	34	Ibid., p. 200.
127	29	Ibid., p. 248.
131	21	Ibid., p. 191.
132	6	Ibid., pp. 17–18.
134	19	Ibid., pp. 246–48.

PAGE   LINE

6   Themes of Dissent

138   1   Eric Hoffer, The True Believer (New York: Harper & Row, 1951), p. 13.

11   Ibid., p. 44.

30   Abbie Hoffman, Revolution for the Hell of It, p. 9.

139   6   Eric Hoffer, The True Believer, p. 80.

140   30   Norman Cameron, "The Paranoid Pseudo-Community," American Journal of Sociology 49 (July, 1943): 34.

142   2   See "The Gang as a Near Group" in Lewis Yablonsky, The Violent Gang, pp. 222–33.

145   12   Kurt Lang and Gladys Engel Lang, Collective Dynamics (New York: Crowell, 1961), p. 186.

35   Jerry Rubin, Do It!, p. 56.

148   7   Ibid., p. 236.

149   32   Ibid., p. 87.

150   21   Henry David Thoreau, Walden, ed. Sherman Paul (Boston: Houghton Mifflin, 1960), p. 3.

151   11   Paul Goodman, Growing Up Absurd (New York: Random House, 1960), pp. 29–30.

34   Jerry Rubin, Do It!, pp. 117–18.

154   31   Abbie Hoffman, Woodstock Nation (New York: Vintage Books, 1969), p. 77.

156   9   Lucinda Franks and Thomas Powers, "The Story of Diana: The Making of a Terrorist," five-part article (United Press International; series began September 14, 1970).

159   13   Timothy Leary, Richard Alpert, and Ralph Metzner, The Psychedelic Experience (New York: University Books, 1964), p. 13.

INDEX